Romancing the Chilli
Chillies & Chutneys

Lal Mirch ○ **Lanka Morich** ○
Marcha ○ **Menesina Kayi** ○
Marstu ○ Waungum ○ **Mulaku** ○
Mirchi ○ **Lanka** ○ Milagai ○
Mirapakayi ○ Khursani ○
Pimenton ○ Puvre de Guinee ○
Paprika ○ Filfil Ahmar ○
Spaanse Peper ○ Peperone ○
Pimento ○ Struchkovy pyeret ○
Togarashi ○ Hesiung Yali chiao ○ **Mirch**
Lal Mirch ○ **Lanka Morich** ○
Marcha ○ **Menesina Kayi** ○
Marstu ○ Waungum ○ **Mulaku** ○
Mirchi ○ **Lanka** ○ Milagai ○
Mirapakayi ○ Khursani ○
Pimenton ○ Puvre de Guinee ○
Paprika ○ Filfil Ahmar ○
Spaanse Peper ○ Peperone ○
Pimento ○ Struchkovy pyeret ○
Togarashi ○ Hesiung Yali chiao ○ **Mirch**

Romancing the Chilli

Chillies & Chutneys

Sunita Gogate and Sunil Jalihal

RUPA
PUBLICATIONS INDIA

Published in 2012 by
Rupa Publications India Pvt. Ltd.
7/16, Ansari Road, Daryaganj,
New Delhi 110 002

Sales Centres:

Allahabad Bengaluru Chennai
Hyderabad Jaipur Kathmandu
Kolkata Mumbai

Design, layout and artwork by designatwork, Pune
Photography for recipe section by Vikas Shinde, Pune
All other photographs from Shutterstock

Printed in India by
Nutech Photolithographers
B-240, Okhla Industrial Area, Phase-I,
New Delhi 110 020, India

Contents

A Word from the Authors

We grew up in Pune, where our parents settled after migrating from Belgaum and Hubli in North Karnataka in the early 1960s. The cuisine at home consisted of many varieties of cooked and curried vegetables, salads, pickles and chutneys eaten with chapatti, bhakri and rice. Wet and dry chutneys were an important part of the daily diet and our annual visits to Belgaum and Hubli exposed us to an even bigger array of them. Our grandmother would tell us about how our father would come home from school or college and call out, while still taking off his footwear at the main door, "Akka, what's the chutney today?"

The chilli really made its presence felt in this household! We watched fascinated as our grandfather, uncles and aunts ate raw green chillies with breakfast, crunching into them much like you would a cucumber! Chillies were a part of the lore and legend at our grandparents' home. They were a measure of a person's guts and gumption; how effectively they were used was a test of a homemaker's skills; the qualities of various chillies and which one was suitable for which dish...these

were hotly debated topics at the sit-down meals in our ancestral home. The famous Byadgi chilli is grown in areas around Hubli, and was the undisputed king.

Our mother's family was not big into chillies and added jaggery to every dish, for which they were teased and called softies! When she got married, she learnt to 'man up' her cooking skills, in line with her husband's tastes. She learnt and mastered the art of using chillies in a spectacular spread of chutneys, both wet and dry.

We grew up, set up our own homes, moved to other places, and found ourselves taking our mother's chutney recipes along with us. Our new surroundings prompted us to come up with different 'applications' for the traditional chutneys. So a piece of toast is spiced up with a lick of ghee and a dry dal chutney sprinkled over; flax seed chutney mixed with olive oil is served as a dip with coarse brown bread; tomato chutney sandwiches are a must-have on our picnics - many other such modern day combinations keep the tradition alive. We are sure that chillies are addictive and the cravings for this wonder fruit are passed on from generation to generation!

As we travelled to various parts of India and the world, we were fascinated to see the chilli's march across the globe. There it was, in its many avatars in our villages, in Hyderabad, Chennai, Bangalore; in China, South East Asia, Africa. The Mexican chilli had overrun the USA, and 'hot' Asian influence was evident in Europe. Today no one eats pizza without spicing it up with chilli flakes. And Spicy Bombay Masala chivda is replacing pretzels in bars around London. Chilli vodka cocktail drinks leave the world shaken as well as stirred! All this had to be documented. We decided to track the chilli as well as keep the memory of our mother's culinary skills alive.

So here we are with *Romancing the Chilli*, sharing our passion, our journeys and our Amma's recipes. Tracing the lineage of the chilli through the centuries, unearthing various fun facts about the chilli and taking readers on a visual journey of the chilli story has been a heady, piquant and delicious exercise.

In Loving Memory of Amma & Paa, who taught us to appreciate the traditional and experiment with the contemporary.

Sunita Gogate
Sunil Jalihal

5

The Conquering Chilli

The chilli is a feisty fruit, that got labelled a spice on account of its powerful impact on any dish into which it was introduced! It travelled from the New World (Mexico) to the Old World (India), during the European voyages to discover pepper and other spices. It arrived in India and China, the largest consumers of chillies today, in the 15th century AD, but is vociferously claimed to be part of these ancient cultures for over 2000 years!

The chilli has criss-crossed the continents over a few centuries and made its presence felt in world cuisines. The indomitable march of the chilli changed the course of the political map of the world and dominated world trade for many centuries. The journey of the chilli is synonymous with these conquests. Also, the fruit has changed palates around the world and got everybody around the world to spice up their cuisines.

In this sense, the chilli has proved to be quite the roving ambassador, bringing the world that much closer together. Three quarters of the world population consumes chillies on a regular basis, making it the most widely used

A chilli farmer from Dharwad, India

6

Central and South America

seasoning in the world.

The spice or fruit is known by its Spanish name chile, or chilli as it is called in Asia, but is called "pepper" in the Americas.

'Chile peppers' are known to have been a part of the human diet in the Americas since 7500 BC. It is one of the first cultivated crops in the Americas that is self-pollinating. There is evidence that chile peppers were domesticated in different parts of South and Central America. Ancient Americans were cultivating chiles 1500 years ago, indicating that the spicy, hot cuisine of modern Mexico has a long history. Archaeologists examining soil layers have found that inhabitants of Mexican cave settlements grew and stored at least ten different kinds of chile peppers. They also found that both fresh and dried peppers were used by ancient peoples.

Early reference to a chilli in a Mexican Codex

Chilapan, from chilli + apan, meaning 'at the water of chiles'. The picture of a chile pepper provides the first root chilli, while the ending apan, meaning 'place of water', is provided by water in a canal.

Excavations in areas in Guila Naquitz and Silvia's Cave near Mitla in the southern Mexican state of Oaxaca have revealed that the ancient Americans were using both fresh and dried chiles in their diet. Remains of food found in caves used as temporary camps and storage areas by Zapotec - speaking people have also provided clues supporting this view. A site at Guila Naquitz has plant remains dating back nearly 10,000 years, pointing to the cultivation of corn, beans, avocados, squash as well as chiles over many centuries. In an earlier study, the same researchers found evidence that chiles were used in cooking in Ecuador some 6,000 years ago. Chiles were used in the pre-Columbian New World to impart flavour and spiciness to food. They were common to the diets of the civilizations of the Incas, Olmecs, Toltecs, Mayans and

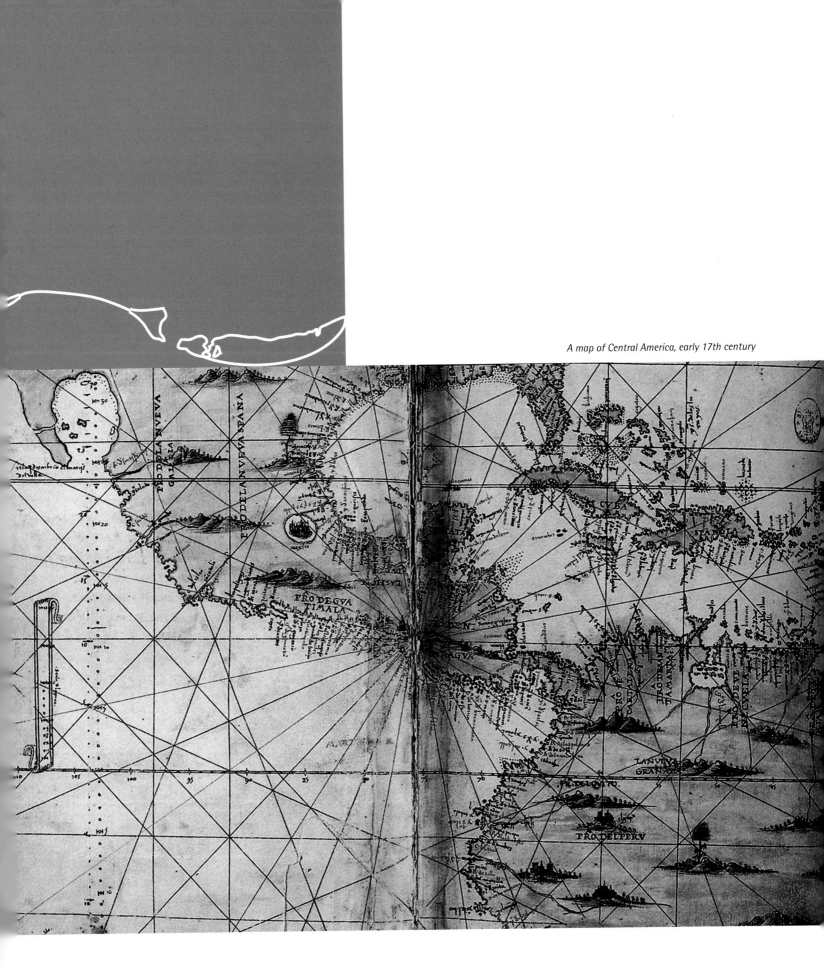

A map of Central America, early 17th century

9

Aztecs.

Hundreds of varieties, including Serrano, Habanero and Jalapeno, are a global identity of the chilli in Mexico and hundreds of relishes and salsas are a daily part of Mexican meals even today.

Christopher Columbus was one of the first Europeans to encounter the chilli (in the Caribbean) in 1492. He called them 'peppers' because of their similarity in taste and effect (though not in appearance) with the Old World black pepper. Diego Álvarez Chanca, a physician on Columbus's second voyage to the West Indies in 1493, brought the first chile peppers to Spain, and first wrote about their medicinal effects in 1494.

While Africa, India and Asia quickly adopted the chilli, Europe seemed reluctant to use it as anything more than a curiosity or an

Voyager's discovery
and its journeys

Diego Álvarez Chanca's statue in Barcelona

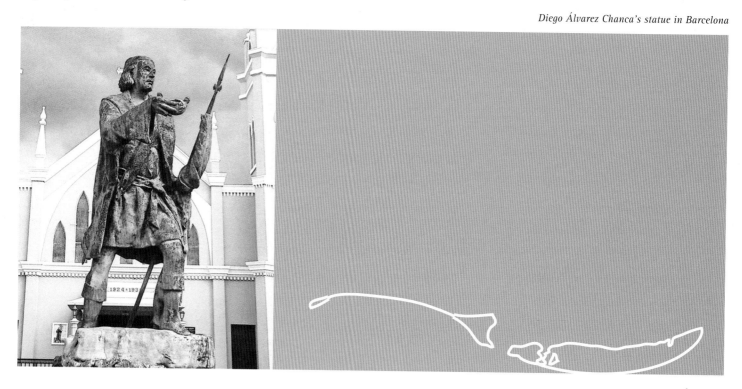

ornamental plant.

From Spain, the chilli travelled to Antwerp, then to Italy in 1526, and on to England in 1548. Curiously, the chilli did not reach Eastern Europe through trade with other Europeans.

There are a number of similar but competing theories as to how the chilli did reach Eastern Europe:

■ Muslim merchants may have brought the chilli from India through the Persian Gulf via Alexandria and then north into Eastern Europe.

■ Alternatively, the Turks could have brought chillies from Asia and then transported them through the Persian Gulf, Asia Minor, and the Black Sea into Hungary, which they conquered in 1526. From Hungary, the chilli then probably moved to Germany.

■ A third possibility is that the Portuguese exported chillies from Hormuz, one of their colonies in the Persian Gulf, to Eastern Europe, as a cheaper alternative to black pepper.

Interestingly, it was not until 1868 that Europeans learnt that chillies were not originally from India. Since then, in the last few decades, Indian curries and bright red Chicken Tikka Masala have become a ubiquitous, many-times-a-week meal for most people in Britian.

World map - Chilli Voyage

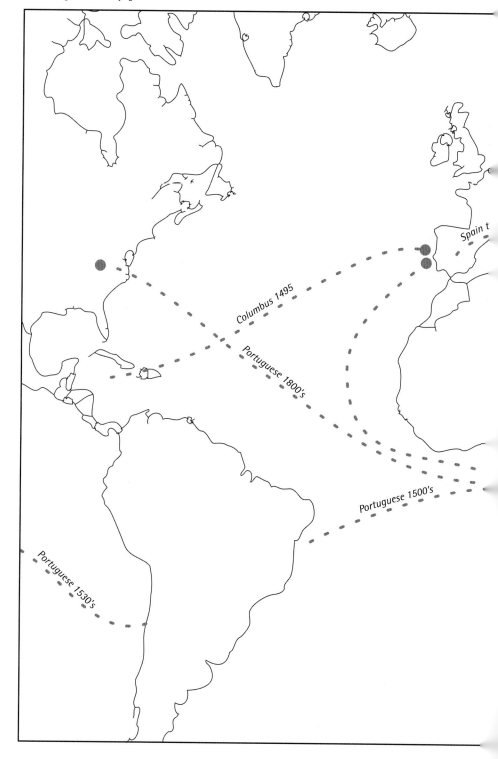

12

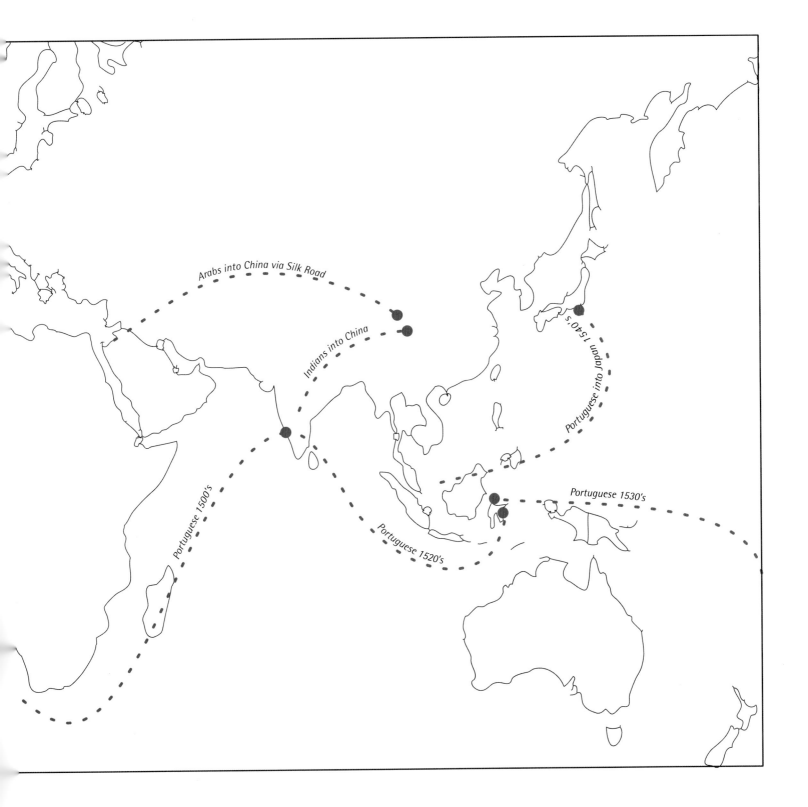

Arabs into China via Silk Road

Indians into China

Portuguese into Japan 1540's

Portuguese 1500's

Portuguese 1520's

Portuguese 1530's

The chilli travelled to India with the Portuguese who brought it from their South American conquests to the shores of India. The chilli arrived in India on the coasts of modern day Goa around 1498 and quickly spread through the subcontinent. It rapidly replaced the peppercorn that had up until then added spice to Indian cuisine. Interestingly, many Indian names for the chilli in south Indian languages have the word for 'pepper' in them. The evolution of many regional cuisines of the subcontinent was to be influenced by this wonder spice over the next few centuries.

The chilli has most influenced the modern day Indian states of Andhra Pradesh, Karnataka, Tamilnadu and Maharashtra. This region was a part of the Vijaynagar Empire, the dynasty that ruled here when the chilli arrived in Goa. The Vijaynagar dynasty had close ties with the Portuguese and had quid pro quo arrangements for dealing with their common enemies and control of trade routes. The earliest reference to the chilli in Indian literature is by Purandardasa, the Kannada saint-poet who lived during the reign of Krishnadevraya, believed to be the earliest exponent of Carnatic music. He refers to the chilli in one of his compositions, comparing it with Vishnu (Panduranga Vithala), the Indian god; he refers to its property of changing colour from green to red and declares it a boon to the poor.

Purandardasa with his veena

The renowned scholar and aesthete Dr. K. T. Achaya writes in his *Indian Food - a Historical Companion* that the *Ain-i- Akbari* (1590), while describing the great variety of dishes in the Royal Mughal kitchen of Akbar the Great, does not talk about chillies, but only mentions

black pepper as the seasoning or condiment to provide 'hotness' and pungency to food. A while later, around 1650, one Raghunatha of Maharashtra sings praises of the chilli in his book *Bhojana Kutuhala* (the joy of food).

The chilli then quickly spread to various other parts of India in the next few centuries. It influenced Mughlai cuisine much later around Lucknow in the 17th-18th centuries and reached the princely states of Rajasthan, Gujarat and Madhya Pradesh around the same time.

The origin of the chilli in the north eastern parts of India among the various tribes is not quite known. Wild varieties including the hottest known chilli on earth (the Bhoot Jolokia) are believed to have been indigenous to the region, making India an uproven 'secondary centre of origin' of the chilli.

The British came to India and by the 19th century had adopted the chilli into their cuisine. They put a different spin on the Indian chutney, with their own variants of apricot, mango and other 'milder' chutneys. The chutney became an important part of their daily meal along with pork, gin and tea! The Anglo Indians took the chilli to a new level, with their Madras Pork Curry, Dak Bungalow Curry and Railway Mutton Curry - all based on garam masala or red chilli powder.

Over the last few centuries, the chilli has morphed in India, and how! Hundreds of varieties are grown and savoured, each district having its own unique chilli varieties. The Indian food industry makes a number of chilli products - chilli powder, chilli pickles, chilli sauces and masalas, and has a 25% share of the chilli trade in the world, while exporting just 5% of its production. The chilli has replaced pepper as the largest spice export from the country, driven by the demand of the Indian diaspora around the world, and is also being exported back to its region of origin - North America!

By 1540, the Portuguese were trading in Indonesia; soon after, chillies made their way into China. However, it is unclear if the Portuguese were the first to bring the chilli to China. Indians and Arabs were actively trading with the Chinese long before the Europeans arrived in Asia. Furthermore, Hunan and Szechuan provinces, whose cuisines use chillies, were connected by the Silk Route to India and other parts of Central Asia, rather than by coastal ports. Moreover, at the time, there were no direct overland routes from Chinese ports to those two provinces.

Asia - China

The Portuguese trade in Indonesia soon reached Malaysia and Thailand. An alternative view suggests that chillies were brought into Thailand via Malacca or India, with the Vijaynagar Empire's maritime trade with this region. The earlier religious and culinary Indian influence in the region meant close links with the Indian subcontinent and the chilli would have become a part of their set of spices. The Nasi Goreng, Pad Thai and other local dishes added 'prig' (chilli) to their collection of herbs and spices.

Asia - Malaysia, Thailand, Indonesia

During their trips to India, the Portuguese traders stopped at various African ports along the way. The Africans' fondness for 'Grains of Paradise', or 'Guinea Pepper' which has a gingery, peppery taste, prepared them to absorb the pungent chilli into their cuisine with ease. In only a few years, chillies had travelled as far east as Mozambique. But trade was only one agent of the chilli's spread; Portuguese slave-gathering in Africa also played a large part in its spread.

Africa

Rooftop chilli drying - Bhutan

In later years, during the time of indentured labour from India and Malaysia, the chilli was taken into Africa, from which came the now popular African chilli sauce, Peri Peri, popularly believed to be of Gujarati-Indian or Portuguese origin.

North America

Most surprising is the length of time it took for the chilli to arrive in North America.

Despite being grown in Mexico for thousands of years, it was not until the slave trade was in full swing that the chilli appeared in this region. By 1600, the British and Dutch had broken the Spanish and Portuguese naval domination, opening up the spice trade.

However, there does not appear to have been any demand for chillies from America as a result of this. It was the use of chillies in African cuisine that was the reason behind their spread. Chillies had become such an integral part of the African diet that slave traders had to bring large quantities with them on their trans-Atlantic voyages. Also, to maintain the eating habits of the African slaves' once in North America (and consequently their performance), the plantation owners had to grow chillies. As a result, it was not until the 17th century that the chilli had become a staple in North

America.

Cajun food comes from the deepest southern parts of Louisiana and Mississippi. Like the area it originated from, Cajun flavour is spicy and rich, though the cuisine itself was developed by extremely poor people. Refugees and farmers used what they had, to feed large families. Adding chilli to a stew, or a dish, 'stretched' the food so that there would be plenty. Creole food is the aristocratic equivalent of Cajun food with more of a European influence. Cajun spices always consist of three things - bell pepper, onions and celery, very often complemented by cayenne pepper and garlic.

In modern times, and specifically in the last two decades, Mexican food related chains such as Taco Bell, an enterprising American businessman who marketed a Tabasco sauce, the use of chilli flakes with pizzas and the popularity of salsas have changed American palates to accept the chile pepper from their neighbour.

We have now come full circle, back to the 'New World', where people are awakening from a dead-palate era of oversalted food, spongy white bread, and diet sodas to rediscover the chilli in all its glory!

Pizza! with pepperoni, jalapeno and chilli flakes

Facets of the Chilli

The versatility of the chilli, its sweep across the world, its properties, its fans amongst chefs and foodies - throws up some amazing 'Believe-It-Or-Not' facts about the chilli. Here are a few that are informative, that amaze, amuse and horrify!

Its many names
Indian Languages
Hindi, Punjabi & Urdu: Lal Mirch
Bengali: Lanka/Lanka Morich
Gujarati: Marcha
Kannada: Menesinakayi
Kashmiri: Marstu, Waungum
Malayalam: Mulaku
Marathi: Mirchi
Oriya: Lanka
Tamil: Milagai
Telugu: Mirapakayi

Around the World
Nepali: Khursani
Spanish: Pimenton
French: Puvre de Guinee
German: Paprika
Arabic: Filfil Ahmar
Dutch: Spaanse Peper
Italian: Peperone
Portuguese: Pimento
Russian: Struchkovy pyeret
Japanese: Togarashi
Chinese: Hesiung Yali chiao

Advertising chillies in an Italian shop

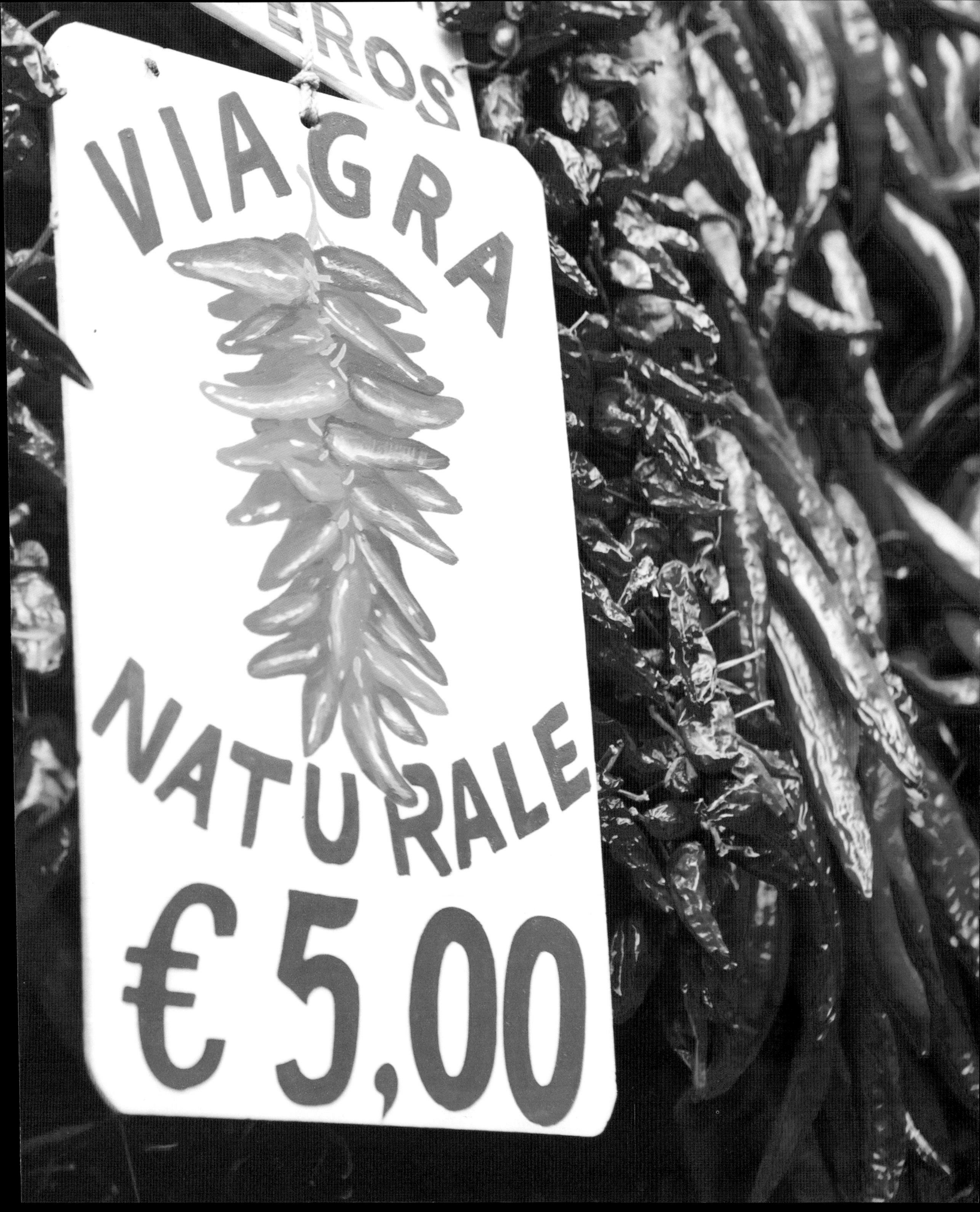
VIAGRA
NATURALE
€5,00

How is 'chilliness' measured?

The **Scoville Scale** is used to determine the pungency of the chilli. The Scoville Organoleptic Test was invented by a pharmacist, Wilbur Scoville, in 1912. The pungency of the chilli depends on the location in which the chilli is grown and the genetic structure of the placenta of the chilli. The pungency of the chilli comes from capsaicin, a chemical compound found in the placenta and the seeds. Capsaicin stimulates the nerve endings in the tongue which transmit 'pain' to the brain, making the body release endorphin.

The Scoville test is therefore based on 'tasting'. The chilli is soaked in alcohol to dissolve the capsaicin. The tongue's sensitiveness reacts to the pungency of the chilli. The quantity of the soaked extract is noted.

Water mixed with sugar is then added to the extract and given to 'tasters' to taste the sample for pungency. Usually, there are five people who taste the sample. To achieve the rating, three people out of five must agree on the pungency. If there is still pungency found, then the samples are further diluted with a solution of alcohol and sweetened water until there is no pungency felt by the tasters. The number of sugar solution drops that are used to remove the pungency completely is the Scoville Index and the ratio of dilution is considered as a Scoville Unit.

High Performance Liquid Chromatograph

These days the Scoville test is done using the High Performance Liquid Chromatograph, a modern machine which has replaced human tasters. This machine is very sensitive to

World Chillies and their Scoville Index.

Bar chart values:
Pure Capsaicin 16000000
India Naga Jolokia 1200000
USA Red Savina 580000
Mexico Red Habanero 400000
Mexico Tabasco 120000
India Patna 96000
India Mundu 75000
Africa Mombassa 75000
Thailand Bird's Eye 60000
Jamaican Red Cayenne 60000
India Guntur 53000
India Kashmir 41000
Japan Santaka 40000
Mexico Jalapeno 25000
India Byadgi 20000
Hungary Hot Wax 10000
Mexico Serrano 4000
Mexico Poblano 2500
Mexico Anaheim 2500
Bell Pepper 0

Chillies at a street market, Castellane, Provance, France

pungency of the chilli just like the human tongue. In this method, the capsaicin is extracted from the dried and ground chilli pods. The sample is injected into the HPLC machine to measure pungency. The test done in this way is less time consuming, is inexpensive, and eliminates subjective rating and inaccuracy.

How do chillies of the world fare on the Scoville Index?

Chillies from around the world vary in pungency from 0 to 16 million units on the Scoville Index. Pure capsaicin is at 16 million units and Bell Pepper at the lower end of the scale is at 0 units. A comparative chart with the Scoville Units of some of the popular chillies of the world is shown on the previous page.

Chilli botanical traits

Chillies are relatives of tomatoes, potatoes, and eggplants, all belonging to the nightshade family and the genus Capsicum. There are 26 known species of chilli pepper, five of which are domesticated - C.Annum, C.Baccatum, C.Frutescens, C.Chinense and C.Pubescense.

Seeds   compressed, obicular and minutely pitted; diameter of seed varies from 3 to 4 mm weighing around 6 mg. A kilogram of seeds contains 120,000-170,000 seeds.

Flower   solitary, extra axillary, sometimes occurs in pairs. Corolla is bell shaped - 5 to 6 lobed twisted in bud.

Fruit   the chilli is a berry, but unlike the usual berries, the seeds are not embedded in fleshy pericarp. The pericarp in the chilli fruit is leathery or succulent which turns from green to purple or red, orange or orange red; the placenta carries numerous seeds. When the fruits ripen, the pericarp begins to dry.

Chillies are eaten by birds (they do not have the receptors in their mouths to feel the pungency) and the seeds are dispersed.

Chilli Chemistry

Chillies are primarily composed of capsaicin - $C18H27NO3$, an alkaline substance (responsible for the pungency) and oleoresins (oils, that hold the colour). The pungency in the chilli is due to capsaicin and other vanillyl amides. The red colour of fruits comes from the carotenoid pigment, of which capsanthin is the most important.

Nutritional Content

The chilli is rich in vitamin C. One fresh medium sized green chilli pod has as much vitamin C as six oranges! One teaspoon of dried red chilli powder holds the daily requirement of vitamin A for the human body. Chillies are also rich in vitamins E, P, and K+.

How are they grown?

Chillies can be grown in tropical and sub-tropical climates. They can be cultivated up to an altitude of 2000 meters. A warm humid climate favours growth while warm and dry weather enhances fruit maturity. It takes 150-180 days for the crop to grow, from seed to harvested fruit. Chillies are grown in a variety of soils provided it is well drained, well aerated and rich in organic matter.

Chilli Plant

27

The chilli's growth is broadly divided into two phases, the vegetative growth phase and the reproductive phase.

During the vegetative phase there is
- ☐ Germination
- ☐ Seedling formation

In the reproductive phase, there is
- ☐ Stem elongation
- ☐ Branching
- ☐ Flowering
- ☐ Fruiting
- ☐ Fruit development
- ☐ Fruit maturity

Chilli varieties grown in tropical environments spend 80-85 days in the vegetative phase and about 75-90 days in the reproductive phase.

Harvesting, drying and storing

Chillies are grown to be consumed fresh in the green form or to be harvested in the ripe-red form. In India, a bulk of the chilli is grown to be sold in its dried, red form. Here are the stages of the harvesting, drying and packing process.

Harvesting: The crop is ready for harvesting green chilli in about a month after transplanting. One or two pickings of green fruits can be taken and the produce is sold in local markets and bought by consumers for fresh table use in cooking, salads and chutneys.

These pickings stimulate better fruiting. The fruits should be picked at the right time neither under ripened nor over ripened. Picking of fruits continues for 2 months. The last lot is left on the plant to ripen for harvesting dried chillies. The crop is ready for harvesting of ripe fruits in about three-and-a-half months from planting.

Drying: When harvested, chillies have a moisture content of 65-80% depending on whether they are partially dried on the plant or harvested while still succulent. This needs to be reduced to 10% to prepare dried spice.

Traditionally, all over the world, this is done by sun-drying of fruits immediately after harvesting without any special form of

Chillies - from seed to market

treatment. The harvested fruits are first heaped indoors for 2 or 3 days, so that the partially ripe fruits ripen fully and the whole harvest develops a uniform red colour. This ripening is done in the shade at 20-25°C.

The fruits are then spread out in the sun on hard dry ground, on concrete floors or on the flat roofs of houses. The drying fruits are heaped and covered by tarpaulins or gunny bags during the night and spread out again during the day.

After 2 or 3 days, the larger types are flattened by trampling or rolling to facilitate subsequent packing into bags for storage and transport. Drying by this procedure takes 5-15 days depending on prevailing weather conditions and produces 20-25 kg of dried chillies for every 100 kg of harvested red chilli fruits.

Storage & Packing: The key issue in storing chillies is to keep them away from moisture. The discolouration of the red pigment of chilli during storage is greatly influenced by the

moisture content at the time of storage and temperature at which the produce is stored. Exposure to air and light accelerates rate of bleaching, so storage in airtight containers away from sunlight is essential.

Packing: Whole chillies are packed in high density polyethylene films in units of 250 g each. They can be stored in a cool, dry place for about a year. Chilli powder is packed in low density polyethylene film pouches typically in 100g packets, and has a shelf-life of 3 to 6 months.

Rats have a great liking for chillies in spite of their pungency, and therefore care is taken in storage to keep them away!

Storing Fresh Green Chillies: Green chillies are consumed fresh. The shelf life of a green chilli can be prolonged to 2-3 weeks by using perforated polyethylene bags and storing them at 7-10°C. At temperatures below 7°C these 'hot fruits' are subjected to chilling injury!

Farm to market

In India, chillies are grown in most parts of the country, with a bulk of the production of dried red chillies concentrated in the southern states.

Chillies drying at a farm near Guntur, Andhra Pradesh

The major markets in India include the ones at Byadgi in Karnataka, Guntur in Andhra Pradesh and Nagercoil in Tamilnadu. Each district in India has its own local market, especially for sale of fresh green chillies. Typically, the route taken by the chilli from farm to consumer is of two types:

Dry Red Chillies

Farmer/Producer >> Village Merchant >> Middlemen >> Commission Agent >> Wholesaler >> Retailer >> Consumer

Fresh Green Chillies

Farmer/Producer >> Retailer >> Consumer

In recent years, prices of dried red chillies at markets in Byadgi, Karnataka have fluctuated between ₹ 40-60 and ₹ 90-180 per kg. Generally production of dried red chilli is in the 600-800 kg/acre range and can be as low as 150 kg/acre in a bad year or in areas affected by mono-cropping over many decades.

Guntur is Asia's largest market for chillies. Normally, about 80 lakh to one crore bags of chillies, weighing approximately 35-50 kg each is traded during the season at the Guntur market alone. The marketing season begins in the first week of February, peaks during the month of April, and closes by the middle of May. The market players estimate that trade worth nearly ₹ 500 crore takes place in Guntur during a season. During the peak arrival period around 0.8-1 lakh bags of 35-50 kg are traded here daily.

Indian Exports and World Trade

India is the largest producer of chillies in the

world, contributing to 25% of the total world production. Till recently, international trade in chillies was dominated by India. However, during the last few years, other countries such as China have caught up. With its high domestic consumption, export of chillies from India is only 4% of total production (around US $ 100 million; around ₹ 450 crore). India exports chillies to a large number of countries spread all over the world, the important ones are Sri Lanka, USA, UK, Nepal, Mexico and Bangladesh.

China has now emerged as a principal exporter of chillies and has successfully penetrated the large Malaysian market, mainly at the expense of Indonesia. The USA has been the largest buyer of Chinese chillies.

Japan produces Bird's eye, Santaka and Hontaka types of chillies. These chillies have a market, but export from Japan is decreasing mainly on account of local demand.

Another significant producer and exporter of Bird's eye chillies is Papua New Guinea. Ugandan chillies, known as 'Mombasa', exported from Mombasa, are well established in the international trade.

The bulk of imports of chillies in western countries is consumed in the food processing industry, where it is used as a colorant and for flavouring. In countries like the USA, UK, Germany and Sweden, considerable quantities of these spices are used in the manufacture of oleoresins and extracts.

Gobbling Up Ghost Chillies

A new benchmark has been set for eating the world's hottest chilli in two minutes. An Indian mother has broken the Guinness World Record after eating 51 Bhoot Jolokias (Ghost Chilli), the world's hottest chilli, in two minutes!

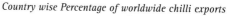

Country wise Percentage of worldwide chilli exports

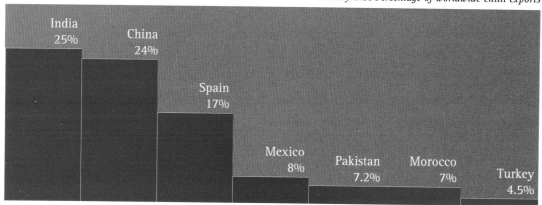

India 25%
China 24%
Spain 17%
Mexico 8%
Pakistan 7.2%
Morocco 7%
Turkey 4.5%

Chillies drying in a Turkish village

In 2009, Anandita performed this feat as celebrity chef Gordon Ramsay looked on incredulously. Gordon himself was unable to eat even a single one! Anandita felt terrible soon after but it wasn't the fiery chillies that had her in tears; it was the fact that this time she had fallen short of her previous record!

In 2006, Anandita had entered the Limca Book of Records by eating 60 Bhoot Jolokias in two minutes and rubbing 12 chillies into her eyes in one minute flat. Since then she has practised this in an attempt to enter the Guinness World Records. The earlier record holder was South Africa's Anita Crafford, who created a record by eating eight jalapenos in a minute in 2002.

Bhut Jolokia from Assam

Chilli Festivals and Contests

A number of chilli festivals are held around the world, each year, especially in the USA and UK. Here are a few of the popular ones:

Annual Chile Pepper Food Festival, Pennsylvania, USA. The Chile Pepper Food Festival started out in the mid 1990s and now, in addition to the wide array of vendors and food stands, it famously hosts the Chile Pepper Song Contest and holds a Chile Pepper Eating Contest. www.pepperfestival.com

Benington Lordship Gardens Chilli Festival, UK. Started in 2006, the Chilli Festival is a very popular family event attracting thousands of visitors over two days, offering a chance to buy chilli plants, products and sample foods from around the world.
www.beningtonlordship.co.uk

The 3rd Lakes Chilli Fest, UK. At ChilliFest 2009, there were more stalls than before, featuring a wide range of chilli-related items such as jams, jellies, chocolate, ice-cream, sauces, seeds, powders, chutneys, clothing, plants, breads etc. www.levenshall.co.uk

Cajun Hot Sauce Festival, Louisiana, USA. People's Choice Hot Sauce Competition, Cajun Food Court, Jambalaya Cook-Off, Refreshments, Carnival, Arts & Crafts, Live Music through the weekend mark this festival. There were 15,000 attendees in 2009.
www.sugarena.com

Annual National Fiery Foods & Barbecue Show, New Mexico, USA. Dave DeWitt of Sunbelt Shows, Inc, 'The Pope' of peppers presents the internationally recognised Scovie Awards for Hot Sauce. www.fiery-foods.com

Hot Sauce And Fiery Foods Festival, Australia. Bringing together the best of Australia's chilli product manufacturers, gourmet food, wines, and boutique beers in one location in Gippsland's prime Gourmet Country. www.hsfff.com

Houston Hot Sauce Festival, Houston, Texas, USA. The Hottest Party in Texas - over 75 exhibitors in 2009.
www.houstonhotsauce.com

Fiery Foods UK, Brighton, UK. Held at Victoria Gardens, with live music, cookery demos and fiery stalls. www.fieryfoodsuk.co.uk

Hot + Spicy Food Festival, Toronto, Canada. Features local and international chefs dishing up hot, sweet and spicy cuisine in demonstrations and workshops. Live music and dance enrich the smorgasbord of events which include the International Iron Chef Competition, the Red Hot Market and Toronto International Firefighter calendar chefs!
www.harbourfrontcentre.com

West Dean Chilli Fiesta, Sussex, UK. This cult event has been running since 1995 and brings together devoted chilli fanatics from all over the world, creating a very special hotspot among the nation's food events; visitors can view 300 chillies and sweet peppers on display in the immaculate glasshouses.
www.westdean.org.uk

Annapoorna – World of Food, Mumbai, India. Food Trade Fair, normally held in Mumbai in November. It is a three day fair that attracts vendors from more than 30 countries and includes various product groups from the food industry. www.worldoffoodindia.com/thefair

Naga Saga - Chillies are developing a fan and cult following around the world. Here's an excerpt of an October 2009 story by Chidanand Rajghatta, the US correspondent of The Times of India.

"Nearly a decade after it was first discovered to be the hottest chilli on earth, the Indian firecracker named Bhoot Jolokia, aka Naga Jolokia, has acquired a cult following in the west among so-called chilli-heads. That's right; like Dead-heads, who idolize the rock group Grateful Dead, and gear-heads who worship all things mechanical, chilli-heads revere some of the hottest chillies on the planet. And they don't come hotter than Bhoot (or Naga) Jolokia, so-named because it is native to the fiery Naga tribe, and those who taste it are said to turn ghostly!

Measured at more than one million Scoville Heat Units (SHU), Bhoot Jolokia is twice as hot as the previous champ - California's Red Savina - who it worsted earlier this decade (Mexican pretenders like Habanero were no match). Since then, the little hottie has become a legend among chilli-heads, grown tenderly in hothouses across the country, discussed animatedly in the higher reaches of the spice world, and sold like gold and other precious commodities on the Internet. Last month, there were 92 Jolokia related items on eBay.

Toby, an American hooked onto BJ has an explanation about why Jolokia has become such a hot commodity. "I think Americans are pretty fascinated with things that are the oldest, biggest, whateverest," he says, recalling that he grew up with a copy of the Guinness Book of World Records.

But across US, and in fact, even in Europe (who would have thunk?) chilli-heads are starting to crank them out with increasing success, says CaJohn. Most of the stuff is still imported from India though, from a company in Tezpur.

CaJohn has a whole array of Jolokia products, most of them priced around $ 10 for a bottle. The first of them is called Holy Jolokia, but the rest, driven by the owner's spicy fervor, has lapsed into blasphemy. When Hard came up with a Jolokia sauce and named it Nagasaurus, an artist who did the label for the bottle joked that it should be named 'Naga-sore-ass'. He did, and the sore-ass label now outsells the saurus by 40 to one. Next up, CaJohn came up with 'Kiss my Bhut'.

It's the beginning of Saga Jolokia."

PS: While we were completing this book a new chilli variety, 'infinity' was developed in Lincolnshire, UK which claims to have beaten Bhoot Jolokia by 20000 SHUs. The race for the hottest chilli is on!

Some of the world's hottest chillies

Special Effects!

The chilli, with its strong characteristics - pungency and colour is used in a number of interesting applications. The chilli's effect on the brain and the heart, on the palate and the nasal passages, and its strong visual effect, makes it popular amongst chefs, cosmetologists, doctors and the police and defence personnel. Read on about all the startling special effects of the wonder fruit.

What makes it hot?
Chilli contains capsaicin, an alkaloid substance which makes chillies hot. Capsaicin is present in chilli seeds and its white membranes.

When chilli powder is consumed, the capsaicin causes the brain to release a neurotransmitter called Substance P. Capsaicin is a chemical compound which stimulates chemoreceptor nerve endings in the skin, especially the

Chillies at a Barcelona market

mucous membranes. This makes the brain think that the body is in pain, making the body respond to the chilli. The heart beats rapidly and the natural painkiller endorphin is secreted. When the capsaicin is eaten it stimulates the brain to release endorphins into the bloodstream. The pungency of chillies is felt deep in the throat more than on the tongue.

The colour effect

Oleoresins or oils in the chilli contain colouring principles (capsanthin & capsorubin) or pigments that are used as natural colours in many applications. Oleoresin extracts from red chillies are known to be used in the cosmetics industry in lipsticks and nail polish. They are also used as natural food colouring agents especially in the preparation of colourful meat dishes.

The milder varieties of chillies, typically from the Paprika family, that have lower levels of capsaicin and are below 20,000 units on the Scoville Heat Index, are typically used for colour extraction. The extractable colour content is measured through a Spectrophotometer, and is expressed on an ASTA (American Spice Trade Association) Colour Value Scale. Chillies like the Indian Byadgi chilli known for its brilliant red colour and its use in cosmetics, are known to have ASTA ratings in the range of 150-200.

Stunning effect

Pepper sprays: In the decade of the 1990s, Oleoresin Capsaicin (OC) sprays, better known as 'pepper sprays', began to be used by law enforcement and corrections personnel as non-lethal deterrent agents in the USA. First known to have been used by the Los Angeles Police Department, these sprays are now stocked by many police departments in the US.

These sprays contain a mixture of water and chilli pepper oil. When sprayed on a person, they can quickly incapacitate an individual, causing temporary choking, shortness of breath, and involuntary closing of the eyes and temporary blindness. The 'victims' begin to feel claustrophobic, the eyes and skin burn and it increases irritation of the mucous

Herd of elephants in an Assamese field, India

membranes, causing the eyes and mouth to water.

These effects are known to last for about 30 minutes. Pepper sprays are packed with chilli materials that are more than 1-2 million SHUs on the Scoville Index.

Chilli bombs

Chilli bombs are being used in Africa and parts of India to ward off elephants from straying into human habitation. The elephants are first repelled by a 'chilli cord' covered with a combination of chillies and engine oil that is strung around the periphery of the fields. If the elephants persist beyond the ropes, communities throw or ignite a concoction of chillies, water, and dung, called 'chilli bombs', in the direction of the elephants. The dry 'bombs' hit the ground and 'explode' in a cloud of very spicy dust, which acts as an irritant that forces them to flee.

The Defence Research and Development Organisation (DRDO) laboratories in India are working on a project to develop hand grenades and other repellants to deal with terrorists and rioters by using the hot-hotter-hottest Bhoot Jolokia. They have already carried out trials for hand grenades mixed with the world's hottest chilli and are getting ready to introduce these into the Indian army's arsenal.

A chilli a day

Capsaicin stimulates the appetite, helps to clear the lungs, improves circulation and acts as a painkiller for rheumatoid arthritis patients. Chillies are thus being seen as a universal medicine that can prevent a variety of illnesses.

An interesting anecdote about late Bhimsen Joshi, the Hindustani Classical maestro and his use of chillies - Bhimsen's stubbornness and doing something that he had decided to do, come what may was legendary. Once suffering from a sore throat, Joshi was advised to cancel a recital. But he would not hear of it. So he tried his own remedy – a fist-full of green chillies which he ate slowly. The pungency cleared his air passages and he gave a fabulous performance. Chillies saved the day and the recital!

Multi-vitamins Chillies have vitamin C and vitamin A containing beta-carotenoids, which are powerful antioxidants. These antioxidants destroy free radical bodies which travel in the body and cause massive damage to cells, nerves and blood vessels.

Detoxicants The antioxidants present in the chilli act as detoxifiers by wiping out the radical bodies that could build up cholesterol and increase supply of nutrients to the tissues. They also act as gastrointestinal detoxicants, helping in digestion of food.

Pain killers Chillies stimulate the release of endorphins that are natural pain killers. They help to relieve pain caused due to shingles (Herpes Zoster), bursitis, diabetic neuropathy and muscle spasm in shoulders and extremities. They also help in relieving

arthritic pains. Many pain-killer balms and sprays use capsaicin.

Antibiotic Chillies help in bringing fresh blood to the site of an infection. The fresh blood fights infections. The white blood cells and leukocytes present in the fresh blood fight viruses.

Brain stimulant Capsaicin stimulates the brain to excrete endorphin and gives a sense of well-being when ingested. This is the reason people get addicted to chillies; it gives them the same 'high' that athletes get at the peak of their performance!

Cancer fighter It has been observed that vitamin C, beta-carotene and folic acid found in chillies reduce the risk of colon cancer. Chillies such as red capsicum have cartonoid lycopene, which is said to prevent cancer.

Heart protector Chillies have vitamin B6 and folic acid. Vitamin B reduces homocysteine levels. High homocysteine levels have been shown to cause damage to blood vessels and are associated with a greatly increased risk of heart attack and stroke. It also converts homocysteine into other molecules leading to the lowering of cholesterol levels.

Lung relief Chillies give relief from nasal congestion by increasing the body metabolism.

Chilli Vodka splash!

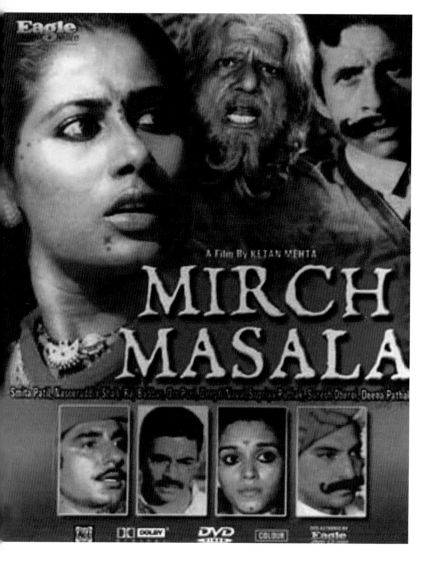

PENELOPE CRUZ
WOMAN ON TOP
AMOUR, PIMENTS ET BOSSA NOVA

They dilate the airways of the lungs, which reduces asthma attacks and wheezing. They relieve chronic congestion in people who are heavy smokers. Cigarette smoke contains benzopyrene which destroys the vitamin A in the body. Vitamin A present in chillies reduces inflammation of lungs and emphysema caused due to cigarette smoking.

Chasing the devil away

In India, the ubiquitous 'chilli-lemon' contraption: green chillies strung together with a yellow lemon, is considered to be a powerful talisman of sorts, to ward off evil spirits and keep them at bay. Most houses, shop fronts and cars in India hang fresh lemon and chillies strung together, to 'protect' the owners and residents of the house from the evil eye. These chilli-lemon strings are readily available in most vegetable markets in India, especially at the time of major festivals. In some parts of India guests are asked to spit into a handful of chillies kept in a plate, which are then thrown into the fire. Chillies are used ritualistically for 'nazar utarna' deflecting the evil eye.

Firing the imagination

In *Woman on Top*, the breathtaking Penelope Cruz plays a brilliant Brazilian cook named Isabella who cooks with such sensuality and abundance of chillies that she renders men on two continents insensibly in love with her!

The chilli has had its effects not just on cuisine in countries that have adopted this wonder fruit as their own, but has also worked its way into popular culture, language, and product branding.

'Lavangi mirchi' is used to describe 'hot' women in Mumbai and other parts of Maharashtra! Anybody with a sharp tongue, is often described as having a 'chilli tongue'.

Many handicrafts and textiles have picked up the chilli motif, to come up with vibrant and sassy designs. Plaster-of-Paris chillies in various colours, tied together like the Mexican 'ristas' can be seen in many souvenir shops around the world. Chillies of various colours and shapes preserved in vinegar or formaldehyde are a big part of today's decor in dining rooms and kitchens of homes and restaurants worldwide.

Many modern brands have been inspired by the dazzle and zest of the chilli. Radio Mirchi is a popular FM radio station in most major cities in India; SpiceJet, a low cost airline in India, has the chilli as a symbol in its in-flight magazine *Spice Route*. Good Earth, a trend setting design house in India, has a range of crockery and cutlery inspired by the chilli. Chili's Grill & Bar is a restaurant chain with over 1,400 casual dining restaurants, mostly located in the USA and Canada. The chain serves American food influenced by Tex-Mex cuisine. The 'i' in the title of the popular food program Chakhle India on NDTV Good Times, is a chilli!

Mirch Masala was a popular and critically acclaimed Bollywood, Hindi movie made in the 1980s and was based on a story of the revolt of ladies working in a chilli warehouse in Gujarat against the atrocities perpetrated by the local official.

Chillies of the World

Ever since chilli seeds and plants left the shores of Central America, they travelled far and wide in a very short time-span of around 50 years (1492-1542). The chilli's adaptability to most kinds of soils, self-pollinating properties and above all its culinary applications had people from all over the globe growing them and producing local varieties. This process of hybridisation, localisation and selection has created an enormous global morphology of the chilli with more than 3,000 varieties of this wonder fruit available worldwide.

This 'genetic journey' of the chilli is a result of local ingenuity and controlled selection procedures in various parts of the world. Variants were created based on control and manipulation of the shape, size, colour and capsaicin content. Thus the Byadgi chilli in

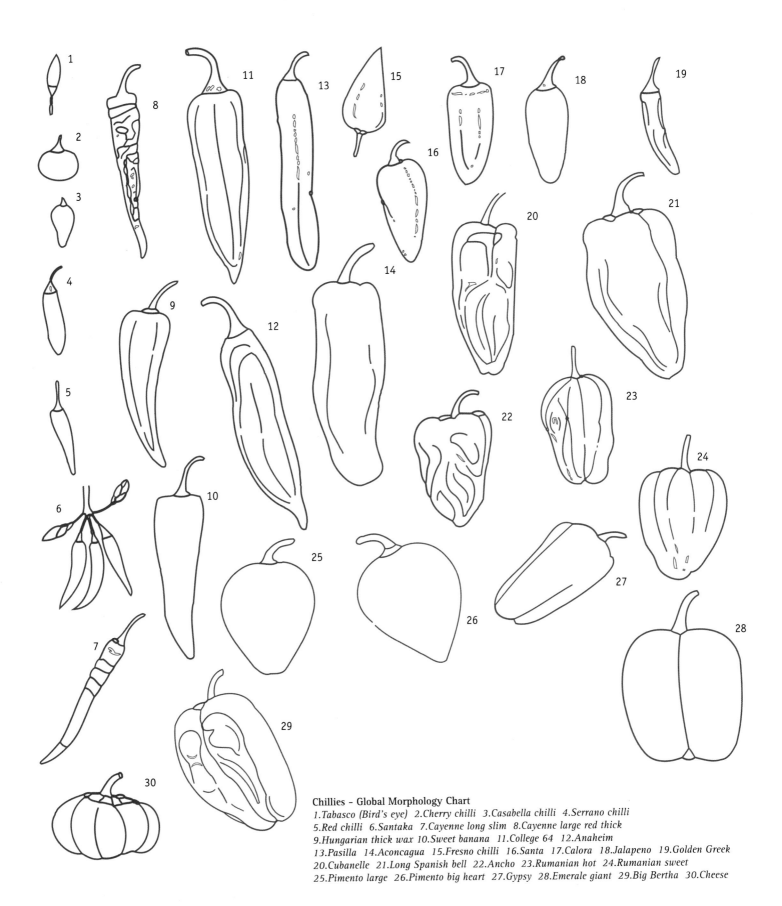

Chillies - Global Morphology Chart
1.Tabasco (Bird's eye) 2.Cherry chilli 3.Casabella chilli 4.Serrano chilli
5.Red chilli 6.Santaka 7.Cayenne long slim 8.Cayenne large red thick
9.Hungarian thick wax 10.Sweet banana 11.College 64 12.Anaheim
13.Pasilla 14.Aconcagua 15.Fresno chilli 16.Santa 17.Calora 18.Jalapeno 19.Golden Greek
20.Cubanelle 21.Long Spanish bell 22.Ancho 23.Rumanian hot 24.Rumanian sweet
25.Pimento large 26.Pimento big heart 27.Gypsy 28.Emerale giant 29.Big Bertha 30.Cheese

southern India is believed to have Hungarian paprika stock origins, which was then developed into a chilli that is known for its brilliant red colour.

Chillies, as described in the accompanying global morphological chart, come in all shapes and sizes and have evolved in various regions around these 'base chillies' that found their way into the specific region in the 15th century.

Mexican Chiles

Mexico has hundreds of varieties of chiles. Many of its regions have their own local varieties and produce some of the world's best known chiles. Mexican chiles generally have an 'acidic flavour' that suits the taste buds of most Americans and Europeans. Most chiles are green (verde) in colour when they are growing and in the unripened state. When they ripen and reach full maturity, almost all of them turn to shades of red (rojo), yellow (amarillo) or black (negro).

The Mexican ristra is the oldest traditional method of drying the chiles. Mexicans tie the chiles with cotton strings also called ristras. There are many different methods of making Mexican ristras. The chiles could be tied in a cluster of two or three, or just a single chile per knot. When hung, Mexican ristras look so attractive, that they are also used for decorative purposes.

Anaheim

Named after the city in Southern California, the Anaheim is a big, mild chile that's good for stuffing. Its skin is a little tough, but it peels pretty easily when roasted. Anaheims

Top: Habanero
Left: Arbol

can be had roasted, cut into strips and thrown into a salad; stuffed with meat and grilled; used in salsa verde; or added to cheese enchiladas.

Scoville Index (SI): 2500

Cayenne

This bright red pepper is usually consumed in its dried, powdered form, known as Cayenne pepper. When ripe and fresh, Cayenne chillies are long, skinny, and very hot. They are relatives of wild chillies from South and Central America. *SI: 60,000*

Jalapeno

Also known as Chipotle. Stuffed with cream cheese and deep-fried as a popular bar snack, or chopped up in salsa, Jalapeno is probably the best-known pepper in USA. It gets its name from Jalapa (also spelt as Xalapa), the capital of Veracruz, Mexico. Harvested at both its green and red stages, the Jalapeno is spicy but easy to de-seed and de-vein if you wish to remove some of the heat. When dried and smoked, it's called a Chipotle chile. It is about 2-3 inches long. *SI: 2500-8000*

Habanero

Native to parts of Central America and the Caribbean, this little pepper packs a lot of heat. For long, the Red Savina Habanero was thought to be the hottest chilli in the world. Habaneros add a lot of pungency to cooking and should be used judiciously. They come in different colours, ranging from red to white-yellow and even brown, but orange is the most common. Great for salsa, hot sauces, or fiery jerk chicken. *SI: 300,000 – 400,000*

Serrano

Spicier than the Jalapeno, the Serrano is a small Mexican chile with thick, juicy walls, so it's a great hot-salsa chile, and is widely available and versatile. It is most commonly sold in its green stage (it turns red and then yellow as it gets riper). Serranos are also pickled or dried. *SI: 25,000*

Arbol

Chiles de Arbol are narrow, curved chiles that start out green and mature to bright red. The Arbol chile is moderately hot, and related to Cayenne pepper. *SI: 30,000*

Poblano

A good grilling pepper that's ideal for stuffing to make chiles rellenos with a touch of heat. Poblanos get fairly big and are usually sold fresh, while they are younger and dark green. At their red, mature stage they are usually dried (and in their dried form they are called Ancho chiles). *SI: 2000*

Top: Jalapeno
Left: Smoked Jalapenos/Chipotle

the largest spice crop in the country surpassing pepper by more than 1.2 million tonnes! Most of the chilli produced in India is consumed locally, with only about 5% of its production being exported. Chilli exports from India are estimated to be 112,000 tonnes, each quarter (Source: Spices Board of India www.indianspices.com).

Jwala

One of the most common chillies in India. Thin, wrinkled, parrot green, long and elastic. Found in most markets in India, consumed in its fresh green form. Used as a fresh condiment in most chutneys and Indian cooked vegetables.

Jwala means 'fire' in Hindi and the chilli is extremely pungent. Jwala is cultivated in most parts of the country for being sold as fresh green chillies and is especially grown in Kheda and Mehsana in Gujarat. *SI: 45,000*

Resham Patta

From the Paprika family. Grown mostly in north India in Gujarat and Rajasthan. Dark red, flat, also known as the Kashmiri chilli. Used extensively in Indian pickles. Also used for bhajias (batter fried chillies) in its green form. *SI: 28,000*

Guntur – Sanam

Flat, red, hot chilli. Perhaps the most popular chilli in India and the largest by volumes in production. Grown in Andhra Pradesh, Maharashtra, the east coast of India and Karnataka. Known for its fragrance, flavour and used fresh as well as in its dried form for chilli powder and in masala powders. The Guntur market in the southern state of Andhra

Chillies of India

India has an amazing variety of chillies, particularly in the southern states. Every district in the country has its own variety. Indian chillies are broadly grouped into four to five categories based on morphological groups apart from local, regional groups and classes in usage in the domestic market. The primary regional classification of Indian chillies is:

- along the west coast (Konkan region)
- of the Deccan Plateau
- of the east coast of India
- of the north-eastern region
- the north and western parts of India

Chillies are used in India both in the fresh, green form and the dried and powdered form. Fresh chillies are used as a condiment in chutneys, salads and Indian sabzis or side dishes. In the dried powdered form they are used in masalas, dry-chutney powders and along with other spices in Indian cooking. With more than 800,000 hectares under chilli cultivation, India produces more than 1.3 million tonnes of chillies every year, making it

Left: An assortment of Indian chillies

Panvel

Pradesh has the world's largest chilli market. More than 1000 tons of this dried chilli is sold in this market, every year.
SI: 80,000

Bird's eye

These chillies are small, very pungent and many of these are known to grow wild in the north eastern region of India and the western ghats. Many of these varieties have their chillies growing pointing upwards and are also called Mugal Mensinkai (Sky Pointing Chilli) or Sooje Mensinkai (Needle Chillies) in parts of Karnataka especially in the western ghats near Sirsi. Also grown in many parts of the Konkan (Goa and Maharashtra), Assam and Mizoram. Kolhapur's Lavangi Mirchi is another chilli from this family. *SI: 100,000+*

Bhavnagari

Jwala

Byadgi

Known to be a descendant of the Hungarian Paprika, grown mostly in Dharwad district of Karnataka close to the Byadgi area, that has been trading in this chilli for more than 100 years. Has two variants – Kaddi (Stick) and Dabbi (Fat). Highly wrinkled while growing as well as in its dry form. Known for its brilliant red colour, high oleoresin (oil) content and high ASTA colour rating of 150. Low-medium pungency. Also used for its colour in various cosmetics, medicinal capsules and high quality natural food colouring.

Byadgi chilli is an important ingredient in spicy preparations like bisi bele bhath, sambar, chutneys and other food items of south India and is widely used in Udupi cuisine. It is also used in meat preparations because of the bright red colour that it imparts. Approximately 25 industries in and around

South Indian Sambar, along with the small
button onions that are commonly used. This is
a cherry type chilli, very hot, red and spicy.
Consumed in large quantities in Tamil Nadu,
Andhra Pradesh and southern Karnataka. Also
common in Madhya Pradesh. *SI: 75,000*

Sankeshwari and Musalwadi
Thin, long, partially wrinkled red hot chilli
grown in northern Karnataka and southern
Maharashtra. Used extensively in its green
form as well as in its dry powder form in the
famous Kolhapuri masala. *SI: 75,000*

Tomato Chilli

This chilli is intermediary to chilli and capsicum. Deep red, low in pungency – grown in Madhya Pradesh and especially in Khammam, Warangal and Godavari districts of Andhra Pradesh. *SI: 35,000*

Bhoot Jolokia – Ghost Chilli

The chilli that has been in the news in recent years and has a cult following amongst foodies around the world. The Assamese word *jolokia* means the chilli. The word 'naga' means 'king cobra' in Sanskrit. The chilli is thought to originate from Nagaland in north-eastern India, and was originally named by the Naga people after the most venomous snake found in the region. The pepper's fierce 'bite' is akin to the venom of a king cobra. It's also known as Naga Morich in Bangladesh and Bih Jolokia in the Indian state of Assam. Ripe chillies are 60 to 85 mm (2.4 to 3.3 in) long and 25 to 30 mm (1.0 to 1.2 in) wide with an orange or red colour. They are similar in appearance to the habanero pepper, but have a rougher, dented skin.

In 2000, scientists at India's Defence Research Laboratory (DRL) reported a rating of 855,000 units on the Scoville Index and in 2004 an Indian company obtained a rating of 1,041,427 units through HPLC analysis. This makes it almost twice as hot as the Red Savina pepper which was thought to be the hottest chilli in the world for a long time.

This chilli needs to be handled with care, often with tongs and is typically sold in Assamese markets in fours, thats all you'll ever need for your capsaicin needs! *SI: 1,200,000*

Bhoot Jolokia in a Kohima market, Nagaland, India

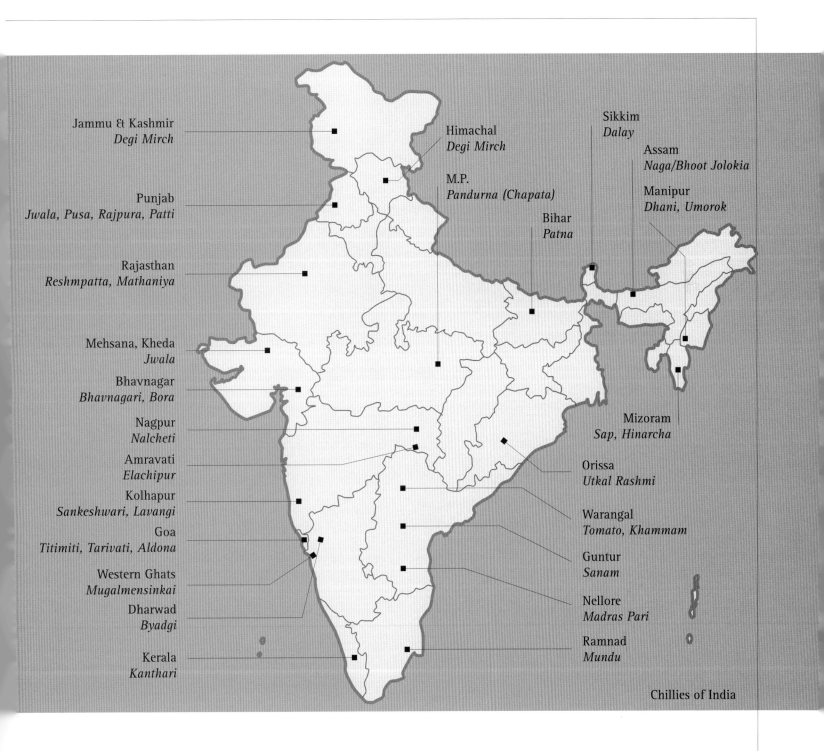

Jammu & Kashmir
Degi Mirch

Himachal
Degi Mirch

Sikkim
Dalay

Assam
Naga/Bhoot Jolokia

Punjab
Jwala, Pusa, Rajpura, Patti

M.P.
Pandurna (Chapata)

Manipur
Dhani, Umorok

Bihar
Patna

Rajasthan
Reshmpatta, Mathaniya

Mehsana, Kheda
Jwala

Bhavnagar
Bhavnagari, Bora

Nagpur
Nalcheti

Mizoram
Sap, Hinarcha

Amravati
Elachipur

Orissa
Utkal Rashmi

Kolhapur
Sankeshwari, Lavangi

Warangal
Tomato, Khammam

Goa
Titimiti, Tarivati, Aldona

Guntur
Sanam

Western Ghats
Mugalmensinkai

Nellore
Madras Pari

Dharwad
Byadgi

Ramnad
Mundu

Kerala
Kanthari

Chillies of India

Map not to scale

59

Clockwise from top left
Kashmiri, Jalapeno, Serrano, Guntur fresh
Chilli flakes, Habanero, Bird's eye

North East & South East Asia

Chinese – Hunan

Most Chinese cooking styles, as a rule of thumb, avoid too much spice; especially southern Chinese (Cantonese) recipes. In central China (Sichuan and Hunan province), however, chillies and garlic are very popular and used in large amounts.

Korean

Thin, long, tapered to a slight blunt point. Used extensively in Korean sauces and the signature dish of Korea – Kimchi.

Japanese – Santaka

Pungent variety with pods that grow erect. In Japan, chillies are used less often than in any other Asian country, but are used in some of their soups.

Thai – Bird's Eye

No Thai dish is complete without the use of red 'Bird's' eye chillies. Cut into thin angled pieces, they are added to almost every Thai dish. Prig is the Thai name for chilli. Thai chillies are from the Bird's eye varities of the chilli family.

European Chillies

European Paprika

The most common chilli in Hungary, Germany and the Balkans. This chilli grows easily in most parts of the world and its variants can be found in USA, India and Africa. It's known for its brilliant colour and sweetish taste.
SI : 8000

Japanese Santaka

Korean

Italian Lombardi

African Peri Peri

Hungarian – Yellow Wax

Italian Lombardi

Of all the nations that embraced the chilli in Europe, Italy was the first and still is at the forefront in its use. Italian sausages, pickled chillies, tomato mozzarella all use the Lombardi chilli. A great chilli in size, shape and texture for canning and bottling.

Hungarian – Yellow Wax

The Hungarian Yellow Wax is perfect for pickling and stuffing. It can reach 8 inches in length if watered well. It is mild enough to eat like an apple and warm enough to induce a small endorphin rush. It has a waxy finish, hence its name. Popped into a solution of 5% vinegar, sugar, water, dill and spices they are irresistible.

Hungarian – Pimento

This is a type of pimento (or pimiento) pepper, which is often found stuffed in green olives. It is a large, sweet red pepper, similar to a bell but with an extra-thick, juicy wall. The skin comes off easily, so this is an ideal pepper for roasting. It's also great to eat raw with dip.

The pimento was originally cut into small pieces and shot via hydraulic pump through the olive, getting rid of the pit to complement the strong flavor of the olive. For ease of production pimento is often pureed and formed into strips with the help of a natural gum (such as sodium alginate or guar gum). Pimento Cheese is another popular application of this chilli. *SI: 10,000*

Spain – Pimento de Padron

This pepper is a specialty grown in Galicia in northern Spain. It is traditionally eaten as a simple tapas, fried in olive oil and tossed with salt; it is harvested young and small, with a tender skin and no mature seeds, so it's perfect for eating whole, bitten right off the stem. It is generally mild with a nutty flavour, but it gets hotter as it matures.
SI: 8,000

African Chillies

African - Piri Piri

African Bird's eye (or African devil or African red devil) grows both wild and domesticated. The plants are usually very bushy and grow in height to 45-120 centimetres, with leaves of 4-7 cm length and 1.3-1.5 cm width. The fruits are generally tapered to a blunt point and measure up to 2.5 centimeters long. Immature pod colour is green, mature colour is bright red or purple. Piri-piri, peri-peri or peli-peli is the name used in Mozambique and Angola to describe the African Bird's eye chili.
SI: 50,000 – 75,000

Modern Hybrids – Application Specific chillies

With the new found interest in chillies worldwide, a number of universities and private enterprises around the world are working on new chilli variants. Prominent amongst these are the Defence Research Laboratory at Tezpur in India (http://www.drdo.com/labs/drl/), New Mexico State University has a Chile pepper institute (http://www.chilepepperinstitute.org/), Luoyang Chilli Research Institute (www.ccne.mofcom.gov.cn/51644) in China and private organisations such as Syngenta (www.syngenta.co.in) and Sarpan Hybrid Seeds in India (http://www.sarpan.com/)

While working on this book, we spent many hours with Dr. N B Gadaggimath, a PhD in horticultural sciences and who has been studying the chilli and its applications for more than two decades. In his farm and R&D centre located just outside Dharwad, Karnataka, India, Dr Gadaggimath has a collection of more than 10,000 stocks or gene pools of various fruits, vegetables and flowers. His collection of chilli stocks exceeds 2000. He has done extensive amount of research on developing Application Specific Chillies that suit Indian weather conditions. He has mastered the art and science of selective hybridization, enhancing the good qualities of specific chillies and producing commercial variants that increase production, enhance capsaicin content or ASTA colour ratings. 'This is our family's passion,' he says, and has studied most chillies of the world and worked with them to produce some interesting variants. 'Its the most versatile fruit and has endless applications, is rich in antioxidants and should be promoted in a big way' he says, as he reminisces over all the work he has done right since working on his PhD thesis at the University of Agricultural Sciences at Dharwad. Sarpan Hybrid Seeds, a company run by him and his family for many decades, is one of the leading R & D driven seed companies in India.

He has instituted plant breeding and improvement programmes, field trials and produced promising material for use in growing application specific chillies.

Whole Fruit Canning & Discing of fruits –
Based on the Italian Lombardi chilli, these

Sarpan Kesar Chilli

Sarpan Paprika

Right: Sarpan Madhu Haldi

64

Indian Chilli pickles

chillies maintain their crispness/texture when preserved and are of a specific size and shape; exactly 100 will fit into a standard bottle. (SAHRC Hybrid SL-22, Jalapeno SJ-21)

Natural Organic Colour and Oleoresins – An improved version of the Byadgi chilli, from the Paprika group. Improved colour ratings from 180 to 280 ASTA, far superior to the 150 ASTA of the now genetically contaminated Byadgi.

Spice & Condiment Quality – Chillies that are low seeded, medium pungent, high colour and that retain their colour after drying. Colour and Pungency 'toned' chillies much like 'Milk Fat Toning'.

Pickling or Achar Chillies for Chutneys – To meet the huge export demand for Indian achars (chilli pickles) and chutney in Europe. The focus is to have chillies that will be cylindrical, thick skinned, juicy, spicy and that won't become 'leathery' on preservation.

Some chillies are suited for chilli vinegar, a big part of Chinese cuisine.

Medicinal Qualities – Medical and pharmaceutical studies in recent years have revealed the rich medicinal qualities found in fresh green chillies. High level of antioxidants and a rich source of vitamin C. Some of these chillies such as Madhu, Haldi, Kesar have been developed to carry high level of antioxidants.

Sweet Chillies Chillies that are 'sweet' (with 0 capsaicin content) and come in various shapes and colours – bullets, cherry, bell-flower, cones and lemon yellow, orange, pale green, purple and white! These chillies can be consumed fresh and complement a fresh salad well with their sweetness and brilliant colours. With their high levels of antioxidants and vitamin C, they could be the ideal garnish to Caesar Salad or Tabouleh!

Dr Gaddagimath's dream is to have school children take the sweet chilli to school and enjoy them like an Indian sweet or like their favourite chocolates!!

Chilling Cuisines of the World

Chillies are a major part of the cuisine in many countries around the world. Mexican, Asian (Chinese, Indian, Japanese, South East Asian) and African cuisine have been particularly influenced by the chilli. Their cuisines are woven around the chilli where chillies of all colours are used in all forms- fresh and dry, smoked, roasted and fried.

In Europe, traditionally only Mediterranean countries and Hungary have had much of a chilli tradition, though food is rarely really fiery even in these countries. Consequently, there are only a few particular chilli cultivars in Europe. The fiery Piri-Piri, an African variety is sold almost exclusively in pickled or paste form. Other hot chillies are mostly used dried, e.g., the piment d'espelette from Pays Basque in France, or the South Italian pepperoncino. Recent (Asian) influences have brought the chilli into Europe. Italian pizzas are eaten with chilli flakes and chicken tikka masala is arguably a national dish of the United Kingdom!

At it's heart, traditional Mexican cuisine is the permutations and preparations of chiles.

Mexican Salsa

Tamales, tacos, rellenos, moles, tortillas, frijoles, enchiladas, etc. are all tempered by chiles. While each region of Mexico has its specialties, the chile is omnipresent.

In Thailand, 'curry pastes' (prik kaeng or prik gaeng) are ground mixtures of chillies with other fresh spices. Chilli-based table condiments are almost ubiquitous in Thailand: nam pla prik (fish sauce with finely chopped green chillies), prik dong (chopped red chiles in vinegar) and prik phom (red chilli powder) allow each diner to adjust spiciness. These three chilli condiments, plus white sugar and ground toasted peanuts, make up the standard set of 'five flavours' which is offered even in very cheap restaurants and at family tables.

In Indonesia, a red hot chilli sauce, sambal, is provided at the table to adjust pungency level to one's personal taste. Sambal may consist simply of mashed, salted chillies (sambal ulek), but may also be fried or enhanced with shrimp paste, nuts or other spices; a popular recipe is sambal bajak.

Most Chinese cooking styles, as a rule of thumb, avoid too much spiciness; especially southern Chinese (Cantonese) recipes. In Central China (Sichuan and Hunan province), however, chillies and garlic are very popular and used in astonishing amounts. Dried red chillies are often fried in hot oil until dark brown, the oil then used to prepare stir-fries. Another method of using chillies is doubanjiang (hot black bean paste), a fiery paste prepared from chillies, garlic and soy beans by fermentation. An example of Sichuan cookery is mapo tofu, spicy minced pork with bean cheese. For this dish, the pork is stir-fried

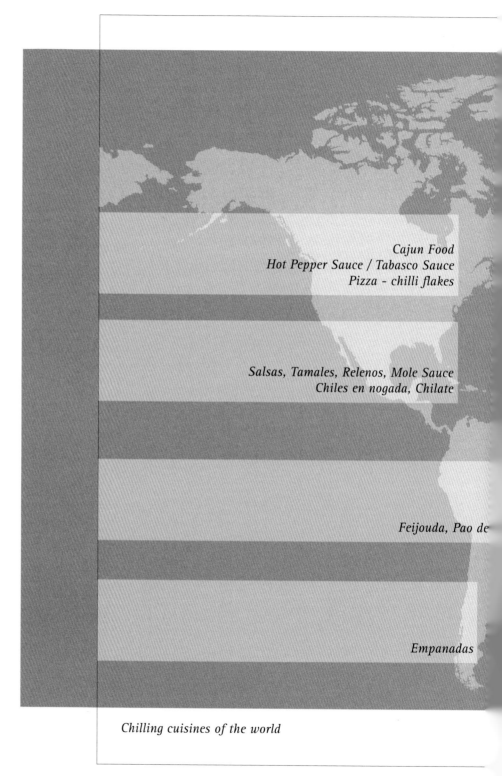

Cajun Food
Hot Pepper Sauce / Tabasco Sauce
Pizza - chilli flakes

Salsas, Tamales, Relenos, Mole Sauce
Chiles en nogada, Chilate

Feijouda, Pao de

Empanadas

Chilling cuisines of the world

70

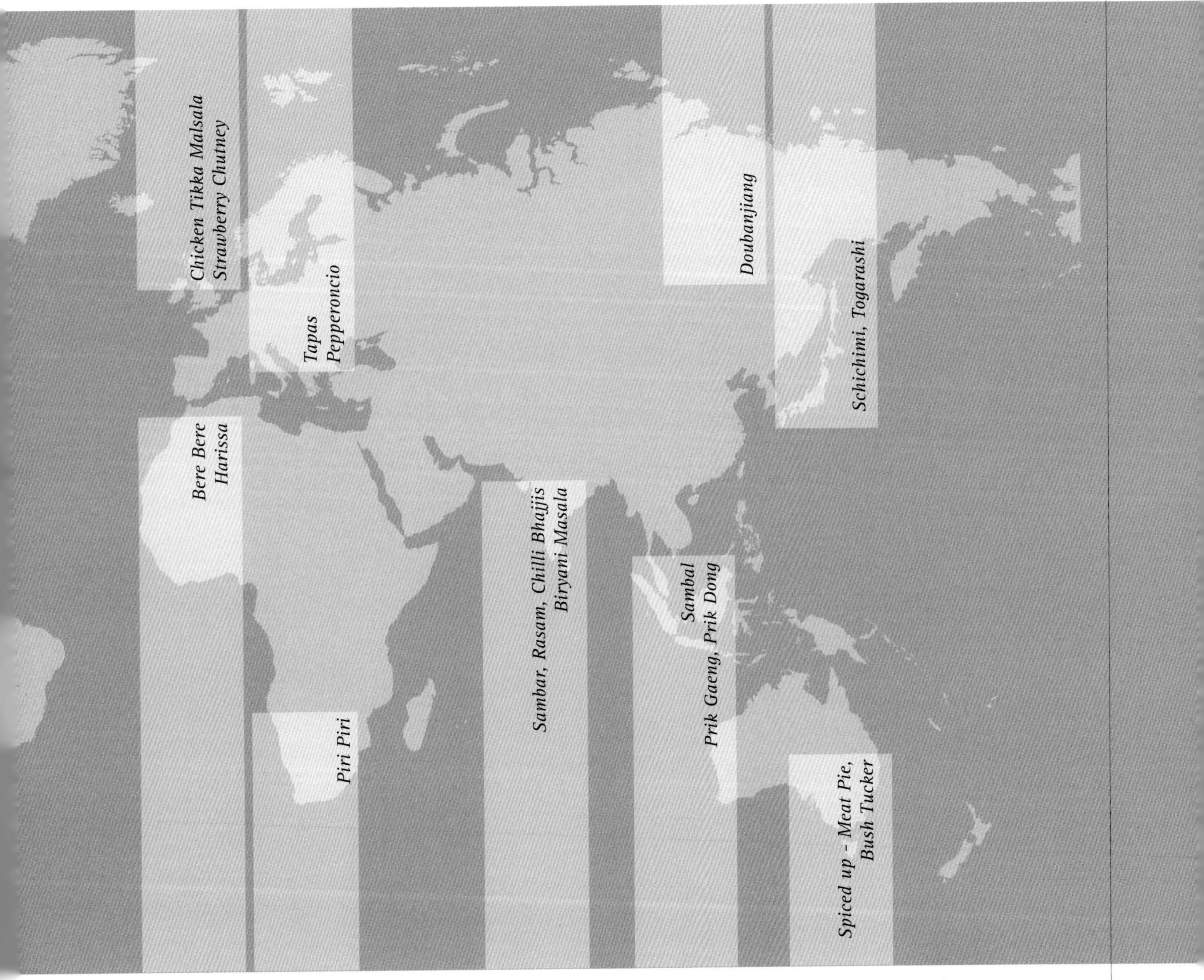

Chicken Tikka Malsala
Strawberry Chutney

Tapas
Pepperoncio

Doubanjiang

Bere Bere
Harissa

Schichimi, Togarashi

Sambar, Rasam, Chilli Bhajis
Biryani Masala

Sambal
Prik Gaeng, Prik Dong

Piri Piri

Spiced up – Meat Pie,
Bush Tucker

together with doubanjiang and garlic and then combined with mild, soft bean curd.

Although Vietnamese food is only moderately spiced, chillies are always available as optional additives at the table, either fresh or in fish sauce (nuoc mam), similar to the Thai custom. This applies mostly to the South; in North Vietnam, garlic replaces chillies as condiment.

In Japan, chillies are used less often than in any other Asian country. Chillies are rarely employed in cooking, but table condiments containing chillies are served with specific kinds of food. Dried chillies, alone or in mixture with other spices (shichimi togarashi), are popular for spicing up soups. In neighbouring Korea, though, chillies are much loved. They are either used fully ripe and dried (a red powder of bright colour), or in the form of a chilli-flavoured hot bean paste.

South Indian and Sri Lankan cuisine use fresh green chillies, which are used in huge quantities for stir-fries and deep-fried lentil snacks. For curries, dried red chillies are usually preferred; three large tablespoons for one litre of curry is not unreasonable. Green chillies are added to the tadka or while cooking most snacks such as upma, idiappam and poha. Chutneys are a big part of Indian cuisine, made mostly from fresh green chillies. Chutneys are made from almost every fruit and vegetable in India and eaten like a salad or pickle as a part of most meals.

In northern India, as well as in Central Asia, chillies are nearly always used dried, except for a fresh mint chutney that is made from green chillies and mint. They are sold whole or ground at the market and are intensively fiery, deeply coloured and intensely aromatic. Usually they are fried in fat so the pungency is distributed uniformly in the food.

Chillies appear in many spice mixtures: Indian masala and sambar podi, curry powder, the Ethiopian pendent berebere and Arabic mixtures. Far Eastern examples include Japanese shichimi togarashi and Thai curry pastes. Other spice preparations are made entirely or at least predominantly of chillies, like the hot pepper sauces of the southern US and Mexico (containing mostly vinegar or lemon juice, garlic, salt and chiles) or Tunisian harissa, a fiery paste of dried red chillies, garlic, cumin (or caraway), coriander, olive oil and sometimes a hint of peppermint.

Mexico

Mexico is a large country with many diverse regions. In turn, each region has its own speciality dishes. Accordingly, chile peppers are used in different ways. Contrary to popular belief, chile peppers are used in Mexican cuisine for the subtle flavours they impart to the dish - not just to make it hot and spicy. Chile peppers can be used as an ingredient in meat rubs or dry marinades for meat or fish before roasting or barbequing or they are roasted and blended with cream to make a sauce for meat. Chile peppers are also used raw in salsa or as pickles or condiments.

Serrano peppers are bright green with a hot fiery taste and are mainly used in salsas. Chipotle peppers are dried Jalapeno peppers that have been smoked. They are often used in sauces to add a smoky flavour.

Chiles being sold in a Spanish market

Ancho are dried poblano chiles. They are reddish-brown in colour with a mild flavour. They are typically used in sauces, and are the most commonly used chile pepper.

Fresno look like a smaller version of the sweet green chiles. They are mainly used as an ingredient in guacamole and dishes featuring black beans.

Poblano are the largest chiles used in Mexican cuisine. They are mainly used to make chile rellenos (chiles stuffed with cheese and then deep fried) or mole poblano, a sauce that is served with meat and poultry. Poblano can be either mild or hot and are dark green in colour with an earthy flavour that comes out when they are roasted.

Jalapenos are often pickled or used in salsas. They turn from green to dark purple, and finally to red when they are ripe. Jalapeno chile peppers are probably the most well known of the chile peppers in the world.

Habanero chiles are the hottest of all the chiles. Except for their bright orange color, they look like miniature versions of sweet green peppers. Habanero are used as an ingredient in salsas.

Typical Dishes made with Chiles
Salsas Chiles are an essential ingredient in salsas, along with tomato, cilantro, onion, and spices. Salsa can be mild or hot depending on the type of chile it is made with. Some salsas are made with a mix of several different chiles.

Mexican roasted chillies

Paprika Cheese; Olives with Pimento chillies

Mole sauce is made from poblano chile nuts, spices, fruits, vegetables, and chocolate. It is used as an accompaniment for beef and chicken dishes mainly for special occasions and holidays.

Chiles en nogada or green chiles are stuffed, fried, and topped with cream and pomegranate seeds. Chilaquiles are a breakfast dish made with eggs and pieces of fried tortillas, topped with cream and salsa. Chilate is a drink made from chiles, raw chocolate, and toasted corn ground into a powder, and water.

India

India is a vast and varied land, a bewildering tapestry of contrasts, cultures and cuisines. If cooking were painting, India would have the world's most colourful palettes. With the historical, cultural and geographic diversity of 29 states, palm-fringed beaches of Goa & Kerala, the snow capped Himalayas and the shimmering Thar desert; the food represents lip-licking regional diversity. Indian cuisine has been influenced by the Greeks, Persians, Mongols and Europeans including the British and has absorbed all these influences like one big sponge, yet maintaining many of its basic principles.

Masalas One basic principle of Indian cooking is the masterful use of spices shared by every Indian chef and homemaker alike. There is a wealth of items in the Indian spice box (the Indian Spices Board lists more than 110 of them). Many of these spices are roasted and ground together into a masala. Almost every Indian household has its own recipes for the masala which can be a combination of anywhere between ten to forty spices.

Five Tastes - Modern culinary practices in India have their roots in Ayurveda, an ancient medical science with its stress on body constitution, medicinal properties of food and the five tastes (sweet, sour, bitter, salty & astringent). Each Indian meal is expected to have food items that cover these five basic tastes. Each ingredient in these items is known to have medicinal properties (e.g. turmeric is antiseptic, cardamom relieves heartburn, coriander seeds are good for urinary complaints) and is subconsciously known to every chef, cook and homemaker.

After the chilli came to India via the Portuguese it was quickly adapted into Indian cuisine, replacing or supplementing pepper in their masalas. Chillies can be bought in India in their fresh, dried, flaked, powdered and pickled forms and can be bought at any market or neighbourhood vegetable seller and kirana store (local grocery store).

Every region of India has its own traditions of how and which type of chilli is used. Fresh green chillies are used as a part of the tadka, along with several other spices and are used to make fresh chutneys, where fresh green chillies are ground together with a few spices and fresh vegetables or fruits.

The coastal and the southern peninsular regions of India generally use more chillies in their cuisine than in the North. The states of Andhra Pradesh, Tamil Nadu, Kerala, Karnataka and Maharashtra are particularly big users of chillies.

Fresh chutneys Fresh green chillies are used to make fresh chutneys, where green chillies are

Tasting chilli sauces

ground together with fresh vegetables or fruits. Typically, local bird's eye chilli varieties such as the Lavangi Mirchi in Maharashtra is used to make these fresh chutneys.

Dry chutneys popularly known as 'gunpowders' are made with roasted seeds, millets, nuts and other spices ground with red chilli powder. These dry chutneys are eaten with idlis, dosas, chapattis, rotis and jowar bhakris mixed with oil, ghee or curds.

Masalas Chilli powder is ground together with many more carefully selected spices to make this eclectic mixture of Indian spices, which is the basis of Indian cooking. Masalas are then used in every curry, dal, chicken tikka, mutton curry or upma, sambar and other dishes that are a part of Indian cuisine. Every region of India and practically every family have their own recipes for their masalas. Xacuti masala in Goa, Biryani masala in Hyderabad, sarin pudi in Karnataka, rasam powder and sambar pudi in Tamilnadu, goda masala & Kolhapuri masala in Maharasthra and garam masala in North India are some of the well known masalas in India. Each company in the food business has its own branded masalas. Each of these masalas use their own recipes with an emphasis on specific spices, pungency and colour. Many of these recipes are fiercely guarded by the family whilst being handed down from one generation to the other.

Chilli Pickles Several types of chillies are pickled together with Indian masalas, oil, lemon juice or vinegar and are served as a part of every meal as the sour and salty taste of most Indian meals.

Masala box -
part of every Indian kitchen

Salads Fresh green chillies are cut into ½ inch pieces and added to most Indian salads called koshimbir, pachadi or 'salad' in various parts of India.

Mirchi Bhajjis Certain varieties of chillies in India, typically the broad, long and tapering ones like Reshampatta, Bhavnagari, Panvel and other local varieties are batter fried with Bengal gram batter coating. Typically enjoyed as an evening snack with tea, especially on a rainy day during the monsoons.

Roasted Chillies The larger varieties of fresh green chillies are slit, filled with a mixture of ground-nut powder, garlic and masala and roasted on an open gas stove or a barbecue.

Stuffed Dried Chillies Fresh chillies are slit vertically on one side and filled with masala and cumin and dried in the sun. These dried chillies are then stored in the spice box and fried in tadkas, which are an integral part of every Indian dish. In South India, this chilli is called balkad mensinkai and is a favourite with curd rice that is typically the last course in most South Indian meals.

Papads, Shev & Crisps These popular Indian snacks have several ingredients and masalas in them, the most important amongst them being chilli and pepper.

Chillies are an important part of Indian cuisine (and almost synonymous with it), culture and traditions. Thousands of recipes revolve around the chilli which has become an inseparable part of India's culinary traditions constantly being adopted, adapted and modified to remain a big part of the its ethos.

Red Chilli Flakes & Yellow Chilli Powder

Fried green chillies - a must with Batata wada

China

Regional cultural differences vary greatly within China, giving rise to the different styles of food across the nation. Traditionally there are eight main regional cuisines, or Eight Great Traditions: Anhui, Cantonese, Fujian, Hunan, Jiangsu, Shandong, Sichuan and Zhejiang. Amongst these, most are not big on the use of chillies, except the cuisine from Sichuan (Schezwan).

Sichuan cuisine is a style of Chinese cuisine originating in the Sichuan Province of south western China famed for bold flavours, particularly the pungency and spiciness resulting from liberal use of garlic and chillies, as well as the unique flavour of the Sichuan peppercorn. Peanuts are also a prominent ingredient in Sichuan cooking.

Sichuan cuisine often contains food preserved through pickling, salting, drying and smoking, and is generally spicy. The Sichuan peppercorn has an intensively fragrant, citrus-like flavour and produces a 'tingly-numbing' sensation in the mouth. Also common are garlic, chilli, ginger, star anise and other spicy herbs, plants and spices. Broad bean chilli paste is also a staple seasoning in Sichuan cuisine. The region's cuisine has also been the originator of several prominent seasoning mixes widely used in Chinese cuisine as a whole today.

Thailand

Thai cuisine refers to typical foods, beverages, and cooking styles common to the country of Thailand in Southeast Asia. Thai cuisine is well-known for being hot and spicy and for its balance of five fundamental flavours in each dish or the overall meal - hot (spicy), sour, sweet, salty, and bitter (optional).

Although popularly considered a single cuisine, Thai food would be more accurately described as four regional cuisines corresponding to the four main regions of the country: northern, north eastern (or Isan), central, and southern, each cuisine sharing similar foods or derived from those of neighboring countries.

Rice is a staple component of Thai cuisine, as it is of most Asian cuisines. The highly prized, sweet-smelling jasmine rice is indigenous to Thailand. This naturally aromatic long-grained rice grows in abundance in the verdant patchwork of paddy fields that blanket Thailand's central plains. Steamed rice is accompanied by highly aromatic curries, stir-frys and other dishes, sometimes incorporating large quantities of chillies, lime juice and lemon grass.

Noodles, known in much of Southeast Asia by the Chinese name kway teow are also popular but usually come as a single dish, like the stir-fried pad thai or noodle soups.

Nam prik is Thai chilli sauce or paste. Each region has its own special version. It is prepared by crushing chillies together with various ingredients such as garlic and shrimp paste using a mortar and pestle. It is then served with vegetables such as cucumbers, cabbage and yard-long beans, either raw or blanched. The vegetables are dipped into the sauce and eaten with rice. Nam prik may also be simply eaten alone with rice or, in a bit of Thai and Western fusion, spread on toast.

Often Thai food is served with a variety of spicy condiments to embolden dishes. This can range from dried chilli pieces, or sliced chilli peppers in rice vinegar, to a spicy chilli sauce such as the nam prik.

North & South Africa

The African continent is home to people from hundreds of different tribes, ethnic and social groups. Common to most of the continent are meals with little meat, plenty of whole grains

Red snapper with Thai chilli sauce

and beans, and fresh fruits and vegetables. The food of Africa is a combination of local fruit, grains, vegetables, milk and meat products, their own traditions and Arab, European and Asian influences.

North Africa - The food of the countries lined along the Mediterranean Sea is the most familiar to the western world. Couscous, the main staple in North African diet, has become a familiar word for many and its popularity out of Africa grows by the day. Harissa is a common chilli paste made from dried African Bird's Eye chillies, olive oil and cumin.

East Africa - People in the inland savannah (Kenya, Uganda, Tanzania) keep cattle, but cattle heads are regarded as a symbol of wealth, not as food; meat products are notoriously absent from their diet. Spicy curries, lentil dishes, chapattis and pickles brought by British and Indian settlers are also a part of their cuisine.

West Africa - A typical West African meal is loaded with starchy foods, very light on the meat, and well dipped in fat. Fufu, a semi-solid paste, made from root vegetables like yams or cassava, accompanoes soups and stews.

West Africans love hot spices - including chilli peppers, probably the only Western world influence in West African cooking along with peanuts, and other ingredients from the New World - and have grains of paradise, or Guinea pepper, their own native hot seasoning. Goat meat is the predominant red meat and its influence can still be seen in the food of the Caribbean region.

Southern Africa - The cuisine is a coming together of many influences. It is put together with local ingredients, including game meats like antelope and ostrich and European contributions from Portuguese, Dutch or British settlers. The spiciness comes from Malay or Indian spices. Piri-piri, a hot red-yellow chilli paste, is an invention of the Portuguese settlers.

Thali - Square Meal on a Round Plate!

Thali, as referred to in the dictionary of Indian Cookery, is a meal consisting of several small meat or vegetable dishes accompanied by rice, rotis, etc. and sometimes by a starter or sweet.

The popular thali is an Indian meal served either in a steel plate, banana leaf, or *patravali* - the ingeniously simple and eco-friendly leaf plate made from 3-4 large leaves sewn together. On special occasions and festive days, in most homes, a rangoli or beaded *makhar* surrounds the plate; in affluent households, the celebratory thali meal would be served on a silver plate.

Each item has its own place on the thali. Salt is served at the top center, right next to it is a 1/8th piece of lime. To the left of the salt is served the chutney (the hero of our book); to the left of the chutney is the raw salad. To the right of the salt come various dishes in small steel *katoris* (bowls). First is the curried pulse (usal) or cereal, next to it is the dry vegetable, then there is the dal and perhaps a semi-liquid vegetable (*rassa* or *patal bhaji*). In the centre of the plate is the first serving of rice with a little dollop of pure ghee. This is followed by chapatti/roti, again served in the centre of the plate. On special days, the thali would have a sweet served in the lower right which is usually a vermicelli *kheer* and *puran*, a sweet cooked with pulses and jaggery; the meal starts with a sweet, with another sweet or two served during the meal. Indian meals do not end with a dessert but with curd-rice or buttermilk.

The entire thali meal is designed to provide balanced nutrition of carbohydrates, proteins, vitamins and fibre. The rule followed is to consume all the 'rasas' or essential tastes, in a meal: sweet, sour, salty, bitter, pungent and astringent. Each taste is believed to be a combination of two fundamental elements of all matter - earth, water, fire, air and ether. The items in the meal are consumed in the mentioned order; the small sweet at the beginning of the meal is the appetizer, followed by all the other tastes and textures. In a special meal, all six rasas are well-represented in the meal, but in a daily meal, the side-serve that provides these six rasas is, without doubt, the chutney. Almost all the chutneys are a combination of all the rasas in the right proportion. For example, the mango chutney has the sweet rasa from the jaggery; sour from the green mango; salt; bitter from the methi seeds; chilly powder provides the pungent rasa; and the astringent rasa comes from the green mango and methi seed combination. Most chutneys provide at least four to five of the rasas, bringing to the thali a beautiful balance of taste and nutrition. That little serving to the left packs a real punch, for sure!

Chillies & Chutneys

The story of the chilli, one that is already dramatic and intriguing, takes on a whole new flavour, when we talk about the chutney family. These potent, pungent side-serve dishes are an important part of Indian cuisine across the subcontinent. Chutneys have their own rich history, as they evolved over centuries, influenced by various cultural cross-currents. India's traditional vegetables were combined with chillies to produce India's own salsa equivalent – the wet green chutney. Dried red chillies began to be used extensively in Indian masalas. Chillies combined with a variety of lentils, oilseeds and condiments produced an array of dry chutneys or podis. And as an array of 'New World' vegetables came into India right up to the end of the 19th century, as the Portuguese, French and the British brought in cabbage, cauliflower and tomatoes into the country, more chutneys got added to the repertoire.

We present a selection of chutneys, wet and dry, from our mother's collection of recipes, some from grandmothers of friends and family and a few that we discovered in our travels around India and different parts of the world. We've photographed them in their traditional settings, but they are equally comfortable in a chip-dip dish, in a Venetian jar, or a crystal bowl! Each recipe describes the procedure to rustle up a quick chutney and provides the cultural context, history, gourmet tips and health benefits.

Chillies & North Karnataka Households

The Northern part of Karnataka, much like its neighbouring state, Andhra Pradesh, is greatly influenced by the chilli. Preparations for functions like weddings, thread ceremonies, naming ceremonies or the onset of summer holidays in every North Karnataka household were bound to start with the grandmothers, daughters-in-law and daughters preparing a fresh batch of masal pudi, saarin pudi, chutney pudi, bisibelebhath pudi, byali chutney pudi and all the other dry chutneys mentioned in this section.

These masalas came handy to quickly prepare all kinds of vegetables, dals, rasam, bisibelebhath, pulses, etc. to feed the bunch of hungry grandkids who had been playing outside, either under the shade of the chickoo trees, near the well or in the lane outside the home.

The kids had to finish the first serving of food in their plates and take more helpings if they wanted. That's how we all learnt to eat every kind of vegetable and have now learnt to appreciate them all.

The womenfolk would discuss the lovingly prepared food and ask the family 'experts' for tips to enhance the taste of the dishes and the proportions for the masalas. This exchange refined the recipes, added new dimensions and brought in tastes and flavours savoured in other households and matths (a Hindu place of worship) visited by the womenfolk during the course of the year. The menfolk enjoyed the food and critiqued the dishes and they were invariably able to pinpoint exactly which ingredient was either missing or was in excess. The brave palate always of course wanted extra pungency and spice.

The one chutney pudi that was used more than any other was the byali chutney pudi as it was served with a hot breakfast of upma or with a dry breakfast of hacchid avalakki (raw poha mixed with oil and masala). In every household, hachhid avalakki would be served at least 2-3 mornings a week as it is a quick dish that can be prepared in large batches and any leftover can be used the next day. The seniors in the household would have it with grated wet coconut, finely chopped cucumbers, tomatoes and green chillies or with fresh dahi.

This food that we ate while growing up probably made us such foodies, and today helps us appreciate spicy food as well as the subtle flavours of cuisine from around the world.

Bon Appétit! Nidaan Aagli! Saukash Houdya!

Most of the recipes make a generous bowlful of the chutney, and the measures are mentioned accordingly. However, for some of the masalas and chutneys/pickles that are made in bulk and stored, the weights and measures we have used are larger, in kgs.

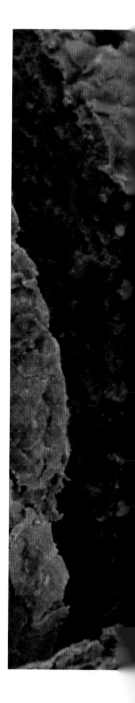

Agashi Pudi - Flax Seeds Chutney

Spice up the healthy stuff

Ingredients

1. Flax seeds *1 cup*
2. Garlic *6-8 cloves*
3. Chilli powder *4 tbsp*
4. Tamarind *one inch*
5. Jaggery *small piece*
6. Salt *to taste*

Preparation

- Dry roast flax seeds till they splutter and the seeds turn a shiny red-brown colour
- Let cool
- Blend together with tamarind, salt, jaggery in a spice mixer

Serving

This is traditionally served with chapattis, jowar or bajra rotis, either dry or with a little cold oil, or mixed with curds.

Easy Variants

Add sparingly to olive oil and serve as a dip with crusty brown bread; kids love it. The traditional Indian chutney mixes well with the contemporary, popular olive oil.

Tradition

This traditional chutney powder has been used as a health food; its health benefits have been recognised in India since ancient times.

Health & Gourmet Tips

Flax seeds have become the most popular source of Omega-3 fatty acids, antioxidants, in recent years. The nutritional and health benefits from flax seeds are well known - they reduce inflammatory responses, preventing blockages in the air passages. They regulate hormones and the menstrual cycle. Flax seeds also help tighten sagging skin.

Spicing up the flax seeds enhances their flavour; the antioxidants from red chillies are additional health boosters.

Curry Leaves Chutney

Boost your haemoglobin

Ingredients

1. Curry leaves *2-3 fistfuls*
2. Urad dal   *¼ cup*
3. Channa dal *¼ cup*
4. Chilli powder *3 tbsp*
5. Jeera *1 tsp*
6. Dhania *1 ½ tsp*
7. Groundnuts/Til/Dry coconut *¼ cup*
8. Salt *to taste*

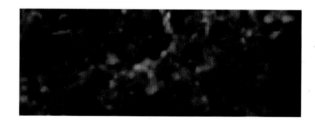

Preparation

- Wash and dry curry leaves. Roast the curry leaves in
- oil on medium heat till the leaves become crisp
- Dry roast urad dal and channa dal
- Dry roast either groundnuts or til
- Let cool
- Pulse all the roasted ingredients together in a spice mixer along with jeera, dhania, chilli powder and
- salt

Serving

Can be served with chapattis, jowar and bajra rotis and curd-rice. Try it mixed in with olive oil with middle-eastern breads for small snacks with a cool beer.

Easy Variants

Try making this chutney by replacing curry leaves with any other dried herbs such as basil, oregano, thyme, marjoram for a more subtle European/Middle Eastern flavour akin to zaatar.

Tradition

Curry leaves have been a big part of South Indian cooking for many centuries. It imparts its unique aroma to upma, curd-rice, fried snack mixtures and dry and liquid curries. Known as Karvepalli in Tamil, Meetha Neem or Gandhela in Hindi, Kadipatta in Marathi and Karibevu in Kannada, it is a must in every kitchen garden.

Health & Gourmet Tips

Curry leaves are very good for the digestive tract, rich in antioxidants and an excellent source of iron to boost haemoglobin.

Karala - Niger Seeds Chutney

Robust, rustic charm

Ingredients
1. Karala seeds *1 cup*
2. Groundnuts *½ cup*
3. Garlic *4-5 cloves*
4. Hing *½ tsp*
5. Chilli powder *4 tbsp*
6. Salt *to taste*

Preparation
- Roast karala till they splutter and turn a shiny black colour
- Roast groundnuts
- Let cool
- Grind coarse together with salt, chilli powder and garlic and/or hing

Serving
This yummy chutney has a nutty flavour and is very popular with the kids. Tastes best when served with curds or a dash of cold groundnut oil. It goes excellently with jowar or bajra roti.

Easy Variants
This chutney can be added to the masala used to stuff small eggplants, ridge gourd or to any curried vegetables to enhance the taste and give body to the stuffing.

Tradition
Karala seeds resemble black sesame. Many Indian languages refer to them as a form of sesame. In Sanskrit they are called ramtila and kalatila, in Telugu ellu and gurellu and in Kannada ellu and huchellu.

This chutney is very popular with the farmers of North Karnataka, Andhra Pradesh and Maharashtra. They often lunch on a portion of this chutney with jowar or bajra roti, especially in winter.

Health & Gourmet Tips
Niger seeds are a popular, healthy bird-feed. Niger seed oil has many health benefits - especially in lowering LDL cholesterol and preventing heart disease. This chutney is good in winter as it has warming qualities.

Dry Coconut Chutney

The ever-popular feisty mix

Ingredients

1. Grated dry coconut *2 cups*
2. Chilli powder *4-6 tbsp*
3. Garlic *8-10 cloves*
4. Salt *to taste*

Preparation

- Lightly dry-roast grated dry coconut
- Let cool
- Pulse together in a spice mixer along with salt, chilli powder and garlic

Serving

Serve with jowar rotis or chapattis. Also a popular accompaniment with wada pav or toasted bread served with ghee or butter.

Easy Variants

This chutney when mixed with curds makes a quick wet chutney to go with jowar rotis.

Tradition

A popular chutney eaten in Maharashtra, North Karnataka and Gujarat, it is a favourite of the gourmand as well as the common man. Also referred to by its other main ingredient - garlic.

Health & Gourmet Tips

Garlic is a well know health pod - good for the heart, the libido, and prevents oxidation of fat in the body. This marvel of nature helps fight bacteria, viruses and even cancer. It is considered by practitioners of Ayurveda to contain five of the six taste-attributes (only the sour taste is missing) needed by the body.

Dal Chutney - Pudi
Spicy roasted lentils

Ingredients
1. Channa dal *4 cups*
2. Urad dal *1 cup*
3. Grated dry coconut *1 cup*
4. Groundnuts *1 cup*
5. Til *¼ cup*
6. Dhania *2 tbsp*
7. Jeera *1 tbsp*
8. Hing *½tsp*
9. Tamarind *size of one small lime*
10. Jaggery *same quantity as tamarind*
11. Curry leaves *2 fistfuls*
12. Chilli powder *¼ cup*
13. Oil *2 tsp*
14. Salt *to taste*
15. Tadka *(see below)*

Preparation
- Dry roast items 1-5 on medium heat till golden
- brown
- Roast with the oil, dhania, jeera, tamarind, chilli powder, hing
- Grind all the ingredients together in a mixer; this chutney tastes best when coarsely ground
- Prepare tadka with 2 tbsp heated oil, ¼ tsp rai, ¼ tsp hing, ¼ tsp haldi and a fistful of curry leaves
- Let the tadka cool, add to the chutney, mix well and store in an airtight container

Serving
This chutney can be served with almost anything from upma, chitranna, masaroo anna, chapatti, roti, etc. Serve with cold oil, curds or just by itself.

Easy Variants
Dry Poha - To 2 cups of dry roasted poha, add 1 tbsp Metkoot, 2 tbsp Dal chutney with tadka, add ½ tbsp red chilli powder and salt to taste; mix it all by hand and serve as a dry snack or with finely chopped tomatoes, cucumber and coriander leaves to make a zesty poha salad as shown in the picture. The taste of this salad may be further enhanced with grated wet coconut and by serving a fresh green chilli as a challenge to the brave palette. Add a dash of lime for the vitamin C.

Tradition
This is a typical North Karnataka chutney powder, always at hand in every household. This chutney has plenty of uses but is most popularly used to prepare the poha salad or 'hachhid avalakki' - every true north Karnataka boy and girl grew up eating 'hachhid avalakki' on pieces of newspaper in their grandparents' house.

Health & Gourmet Tips
Red chillies are a rich source of antioxidants. The chutney assures a tasty supply of carbohydrates with every meal.

Groundnut Chutney

The earthy alternative

Ingredients
1. Groundnuts *2 cups*
2. Chilli powder *3-4 tbsp*
3. Salt *to taste*

Preparation
- Roast groundnuts on medium heat till brown spots appear on the red skin
- Let cool
- Blend in a spice mixer along with red chilli powder and salt

Serving
Serve with chapattis, rotis, etc. Tastes good when mixed with dahi and metkoot to make a quick chutney to go with dosas, idlis, uttapams.

Easy Variants
This chutney can be coarse ground for a more crunchy bite or more fine for a smoother texture. The taste of this chutney can be enhanced by adding 6-8 garlic pods while grinding. This chutney can be used on toasted bread slices as a quick breakfast or snack for kids with its taste of spiced peanut butter.

Tradition
This is a more contemporary chutney made in households in Maharashtra, North Karnataka and Gujarat. Served with wada pav and many other snacks. Groundnuts are a late entrant to Indian cuisine, known to have come to India around the 1800s - the larger Brazilian ones via Africa and the smaller ones independently from China.

Health & Gourmet Tips
Groundnuts are a great source of instant energy. Fresh groundnuts, boiled, salted and tossed with fresh green chillies, fresh coriander and chilli powder are a great accompaniment with beer!

North Karnataka Masala

Putting zing into sabzis and sambars

Ingredients

1. Dhania *1 cup*
2. Jeera *1 cup*
3. Methi *½ tbsp*
4. Til *3 tbsp*
5. Channa dal *1 tbsp*
6. Urad dal *1 tbsp*
7. Grated dry coconut *2 tbsp*
8. Dalchini stick *3"*
8. Jaiphal/Jaiphal Patri *¼ tbsp*
9. Lavang *4-6*
10. Velchi *3-4*
11. Dagad phul *7-8*
12. Tamalpatra (Bay Leaf) *2*
13. Hing *½ tsp*
14. Maratha moggu *½ tsp*
15. Chilli powder *1 tbsp*
16. Curry leaves *one fistful*
17. Salt *to taste*

Preparation

- Dry-roast, separately, coconut, til, urad, channa dal
- Roast all the remaining items except dhania separately, using a little oil each time
- Roast dhania till black spots appear, add chill
- powder and switch off the heat and let cool
- Grind all the roasted ingredients together to a coarse
- to fine powder

Serving

This masala can be used to spice up vegetables, lentils, pulses, or as a spice to cook rice with vegetables. It works well when added to the wet masala used to make stuffed small brinjals. Lends a great flavour to toor dal sambar or hooli.

Easy Variants

The quantity of the ingredients can be varied depending on the level of spice that each household prefers. The same masala powder can be made without any chilli powder and by increasing the dhania by ½ cup to make a less spicy variation.

Tradition

This is a typical and distinctive masala powder found in every North Karnataka household; of course, variations thrown in by every lady of the house add a new dimension to the masala each time that it is prepared.

Health & Gourmet Tips

Every ingredient contributes some health benefit - digestive, carminative, immunity-boosting...

Saarin Pudi

Spice up your mulligatawny

Ingredients
1. Dhania *1 cup*
2. Methi *2 tbsp*
3. Peppercorns *2 tbsp*
4. Jeera *1 tsp*
5. Hing *½ tsp*
6. Chilli powder *1 tbsp*
7. Oil *1 tbsp*
8. Salt *to taste*

Preparation
- Heat oil on medium heat, add peppercorns, cover till they splutter
- Add methi, roast till red
- Add jeera, dhania, hing, curry leaves, roast lightly
- Switch off heat; add chilli powder
- Let cool
- Grind together in a spice mixer

Serving
This is the spice powder used to make saar/rasam, the popular dal-based soup. The powder is boiled along with tomatoes and or tamarind pulp, and added to pressure-cooked toor dal. To enhance the taste of this saar/rasam add tadka or tempering of rai, hing, turmeric powder, dry red chillies and curry leaves and boil.

Easy Variants
This powder can be added to a tempering along with roasted peanuts, channa dal, urad dal and red chilli powder. When this mixture cools down, add the tamarind pulp and mix in with cooked rice to make tasty puliyogare rice.

Tradition
This is another typically North Karnataka masala found in every household and is used regularly to enhance the flavour of lentils. Saars are typically named after the main vegetable that's cooked along with the masala and tamarind or tomatoes.

Health & Gourmet Tips
This spice makes an excellent hot soup, and helps relieve congestion in common colds and sinusitis. It keeps the insides warm and is a comfort food for those recovering from loss of appetite.

Kolhapuri Masala

The macho man mix

Ingredients

1. Red Chillies *1 kg*
2. Dhania *¼ kg*
3. Dry coconut *¼ kg*
4. Tamalpatra *20 gm*
5. Lavang *20 gm*
6. Dalchini *20 gm*
7. Shahajeera *20 gm*
8. Badalphul *20 gm*
9. Dagadphul *20 gm*
10. Badi Elaichi *20 gm*
11. Khada Hing *20 gm*
12. Jaypatri *10 gm*
13. Nagkeshar *10 gm*
14. Methi seeds *10 gm*
15. Haldi powder *120 gm*
16. Rai *10 gm*
17. Til *2 cups*
18. Khus khus *1 cup*
19. Onions *½ kg**
20. Garlic *½ kg**
21. Fresh coriander *1 cup chopped**
22. Ginger *2 tbsp grated**
23. Oil *2 tsp*
24. Salt *to taste*

Preparation

- Dry roast rai, shahajeera, til, khus khus and grated dry coconut.
- All the above to be ground together for masala 1
- All the other ingredients except 19-22 to be roasted
- separately with a little bit of oil
- All the above ingredients to be ground together for masala 2

- The above two ground masalas can be stored separately in airtight containers.

- To prepare the Kolhapuri masala, take ¼ quantity of masalas 1 and 2 and mix together. To this mixture add the below mentioned wet masala and use fresh
- Slice the onions the previous night, spread out on a plate and leave overnight
- In a cup of oil deep fry the onions till golden brown, deep fry the garlic, ginger and coriander leaves
- Grind this together along with salt
- Making small batches of this masala keeps it fresh
- and enhances the flavour of the combined masala

Serving

Used to make chicken rassa and mutton rassa as also the bone-marrow dish; also a number of meat dishes such as mutton Kolhapuri, mutton sukka and chicken Kolhapuri. This masala can be used to prepare usals, dals, potato curry and other curried vegetables Kolhapuri style.

Tradition

This masala is a traditional one from Kolhapur, Maharashtra and was used in the royal Maratha kitchens. Every Maratha household prepares a batch of the dry masalas in huge quantities in the villages and sends it out to their extended family living in places far and near. The wet chutney with onions and garlic is prepared fresh and added to the dry masala when needed.

Health & Gourmet Tips

Red chillies are a rich source of antioxidants. Eat food made with this fiery masala in summer to cool your body and keep away the flu. Use ½ kg Byadgi for colour and ½ kg Sankeshwari chillies for heat and flavour.

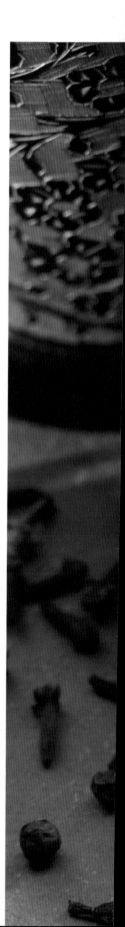

Garam Masala

Nawabi shauk - the Mughal gift

Ingredients
1. Dhania   *1 cup*
2. Jeera   *½ cup*
3. Jaiphal   *1*
4. Black peppercorns   *1 tbsp*
5. Cloves   *10-15*
6. Cinnamon stick   *4"*
7. Shahajeera   *2 tbsp*
8. Jaipatri   *1 tbsp*

Preparation
- Grind all the ingredients together in a spice mixer
- Store in an airtight container

Serving
Garam masala is a popular masala to marinate and cook meat - kababs, biryani, tikkas, Kashmiri rogan josh, etc. Also used to make North Indian vegetarian dishes - chole masala and rajma masala.

Easy Variants
Garam masala is often made fresh, with fresh garlic, onions and coconut milk (in southern India) added to the spices and ground together to make a masala paste.

Tradition
Notice that this masala does not use chilli powder (although some commercial variants do use chilli powder). Chilli did not influence the masalas of North India as they did the South. This is a masala that originates in the northern states of India where the Mughal influence most prominently left its mark. This masala is mainly used in Mughlai cuisine and has been described in detail in the *Ain-i-Akbari* written by Abu Fazal in the 16th century.

Health & Gourmet Tips
A great marinade for cooking meats and barbecues. Meat can be marinated with this mixture of spices with curd. Use garam masala to make a tasty egg curry and serve with hot whole wheat rotis, parathas or brown bread.

Metkoot

That first taste of spice

Ingredients
1. Channa dal *4 cups*
2. Rice *1 cup*
3. Urad dal *½ cup*
4. Dhania *2 tbsp*
5. Jeera *1 tbsp*
6. Lavang *5-6*
7. Ilaichi *8-10*
8. Jaiphal *1*
9. Dry ginger *2 sticks*
10. Chilli powder *1/2 tsp*
11. Hing *1/2 tsp*
12. Rai *1 tsp*

Preparation
- Dry roast the dals and the rice separately till they turn a light golden brown colour
- Grind all the ingredients together
- Store in an airtight container

Serving
Metkoot tastes best when served with soft hot rice and ghee with a little salt and a dash of lime.

Easy Variants
Metkoot can be used to garnish lemon rice, poha, etc. Mix with curds and temper with a tadka for a quick chutney.

Tradition
Metkoot has been traditionally used with soft rice and ghee to feed little children - the mild spice brings them a tiny step closer to grown-up eating!

Health & Gourmet Tips
Metkoot serves as a protein and vitamin tonic for kids. The dals are a rich source of proteins, the spices cleanse the system and add the aroma and taste to this multi-vitamin meal. It is eaten with rice and ghee, which is itself considered an extraordinary 'lubricant' in Ayurveda.

Coriander and Lime Chutney

The ever-popular classic

Ingredients
1. Coriander leaves *1 bunch*
2. Green chillies *4-5*
3. Juice of *1 lime*
4. Salt *to taste*

Preparation
- Blend all the ingredients together in a blender using the pulse button

Serving
This chutney is traditionally served with hot samosas, pakoras, cutlets and parathas. Use it to spice up chaats and bhelpuri. It may be used as a salad dressing with cucumber, tomatoes or boiled pasta. Use as a salad dressing, by thinning out the chutney with olive oil, salad oil or extra lime juice

Easy Variants
This chutney can be made in the same way with a bunch of mint leaves, green chillies, ginger and garlic. This is the ever popular mint chutney, also served mixed with curds.

Tradition
Coriander is a fresh herb that has been used to enhance the taste of curries, chutneys, dhokla and other savoury dishes. This is the most popular and widely used herb in India and has been used to garnish food before the more western herbs like basil, parsley, rosemary and thyme became popular. Samosas or bhajiyas served with coriander chutney accompanied with a glass of piping hot chai is a big part of romancing the monsoons in India.

Health & Gourmet Tips
Eating raw coriander is an excellent way of getting rid of metals like mercury, lead and aluminum from one's body; coriander is also a blood cleanser.

Tomato Chutney

The spicy fresh ketchup that kids love

Ingredients
1. Ripe red tomatoes *4*
2. Til *½ cup*
3. Green chillies *8-10*
4. Onion *1 small*
5. Garlic cloves *5-6*
6. Oil *4 tbsp*
7. Coriander leaves *½ cup chopped*
8. Hing *½ tsp*
9. Rai *½ tsp*
10. Salt *to taste*

Preparation
- Roast the sesame seeds on medium heat till golden brown or till they start spluttering, and set aside
- Dice the tomatoes, onion and chillies into bite size pieces
- Prepare tadka with oil, rai and hing.
- Add garlic pods, green chillies and onion, cook for a few minutes
- Add diced tomatoes and mix well, cover with a lid and let cook for 2 minutes; when the tomatoes start to sweat, remove the lid and evaporate some of the juices.
- Let cool
- In a chutney blender, coarsely grind the roasted sesame seeds, add the cooked tomato mixture, salt, coriander and blend together using the pulse button. Try and keep the chutney a coarse blend for the perfect texture.

Serving
This chutney can be served with idlis or wheat rotis. Kids love sandwiches made with this chutney and sliced veggies.

Easy Variants
Use green unripe tomatoes for a tangy and green version of this chutney.

Tradition
Tomatoes are arguably the most popular vegetable worldwide along with potatoes and onions. Tomato sauce is perhaps the best-known accompaniment seen on every dining table in the world. Another Mexican and Peruvian gift to the world, tomatoes reached Europe in 1550 and were first adopted in Italy as an excellent partner to pasta dishes. The British are believed to have brought the tomato into India around 1850 and it slowly became a popular vegetable for its sour and sweet taste.

The tomato chutney is a modern day tomato ketchup for the culinary adventurers.

Health & Gourmet Tips
Chillies are a rich source of antioxidants. Tomatoes are rich in vitamin E, which is good for the liver. Eat in summer to cool your body and keep away the flu. Use Byadgi or Guntur chillies for colour and flavour.

Green Tomato Chutney

Tangy chutney with the nutty taste of sesame seeds

Ingredients
1. Green tomatoes *5-6*
2. Green chillies *10-12*
3. Til *½ cup*
4. Coriander leaves *½ cup chopped*
5. Oil *4 tbsp*
6. Hing *½ tsp*
7. Rai *½ tsp*
8. Salt *to taste*

Preparation
- Roast the sesame seeds and set aside
- Dice tomatoes into small pieces, cut chillies into pieces
- Prepare tadka
- Add chillies and green tomatoes and cook for a few minutes without lid; the green tomatoes do not sweat as much as the red
- Let this cool
- In a chutney blender, grind the roasted sesame seeds, add the cooked tomato mixture, salt, coriander and blend together using pulse button. Try and keep the chutney a coarse blend. This retains texture and body.

Serving
Serve chilled with fresh coriander and dry chilli tadka. Eat with idlies. Make picnic sandwiches for the kids with brown bread.

Easy Variants
You may adjust the quantity of chillies to suit your palate and you may also add a little bit of sugar if you prefer the sweet, sour and spicy taste.

Tradition
The tomato chutney is a spicy and tangy replacement for tomato sauce with a lot more body and the added taste of the sesame seeds. A chunky combination of Tomato and Tahini Sauce if you will!

Health & Gourmet Tips
Green chillies are a rich source of antioxidants. Tomatoes are rich in vitamin E which is good for the liver. Eat in summer to cool your body and keep away the flu. Use Bird's Eye or Lavangi chillies for that extra spiciness.

Gongura Chutney

Hot and sour leaves; Andhra identity

Ingredients
1. Gongura leaves *1 bunch*
2. Green chillies *10-15 (use Guntur chillies if available)*
3. Garlic *15-20 cloves*
4. Oil *2 tbsp*
5. Rai *½ tsp*
6. Salt *to taste*

Preparation
- Wash and pat dry gongura leaves
- In a pan heat 1 tbsp of oil, add rai and after they splutter add the garlic, chillies and gongura leaves
- Sauté for about 5-7 minutes, let cool
- Add salt and blend well in a chutney blender

Serving
Garnish with the remaining 1 tbsp oil and mix the chutney once again. Serve with jowar rotis and raw onions. Add a few drops of oil on the chutney in your plate and mix it well; this really enhances the taste of the chutney.

Easy Variants
Spread some gongura chutney on small slices of hard or toasted bread and top with finely sliced raw onions - this makes good small eats (a la tapas) to serve with cocktails.

Tradition
Gongura or Gonkuru, the tall plant Hibiscus canabinus, is also called nalita and ambadi in India and kenaf and mesta in other parts of the world. The sour leaves are eaten as a pacchadi or salad in the Andhra region. Gongura chutney or pickle is the signature dish of Andhra Pradesh. The plant fibre is twisted into ropes

Health & Gourmet Tips
Gongura cools the body; this is an excellent chutney to have in summer to avoid heat stroke. The cooling effect of gongura and the Guntur green chillies is perfect to combat the heat of summer.

Ranjka

An inspiring classic

Ingredients
1. Ripe red fresh chillies *20-25*
2. Methi seeds *1 tsp*
3. Hing *1 1/2 tsp*
4. Lime Juice *1 lemon*
5. Oil *2 tsp*
6. Tadka
7. Salt *to taste*

Preparation
- Heat a little oil and roast the methi seeds in the oil
- Set aside
- Grind together the ripe red chillies, methi seeds, hing and salt coarsely
- The quantity of salt needs to be a little more than that for a chutney so that Ranjka can be pickled in glass bottles or ceramic jars in order to last upto a year
- While serving, temper with a rai and hing tadka, and a dash of lime juice

Serving
Tastes good with chapatti, bhakri, poha or upma. Especially popular with curd rice and chitranna (lemon rice).

Easy Variants
Add about 10-12 garlic cloves and reduce the quantity

Tradition
The signature chilli chutney of many a region, especially North Karnataka. In the Byadgi region, fresh, ripe, red crisp chillies are specially chosen in the month of October to make Ranjka for the whole year. Every household has its own recipe and this pickle/chutney is a must on the pickle shelf.

This really basic and simple chutney was one of the inspirations for this book. The deep red colour and the fiery taste of nothing but chillies distinguishes this chutney from all others in this book.

Health & Gourmet Tips
All the antioxidants, vitamins and nutrition of the chilli. The methi seeds are anti-diabetic.

Tokku

Pickle or Chutney?

Ingredients

1. Green tamarind *1 kg*
2. Green chillies *3 kg*
3. Methi seeds *3 tbsp*
4. Hing *1 tsp*
5. Haldi *2 tbsp*
6. Salt *a little more than usual*

Preparation

- Heat a little oil and roast the methi seeds, let cool
- Grind together the green tamarind, chillies, salt, hing and turmeric powder in a wet grinder
- Store in glass or ceramic pickling jars
- Tokku is made to last for a year, hence the extra salt

Serving

Add tadka to a small quantity before serving. This chutney can be served with upma, poha, curd rice, chapatti and bhakri. Add tokku to curds, mix well and enjoy as a dip.

Easy Variants

Use this chutney to make a slurpy, sour, sweet and pungent rassa, by dropping a few lumps of tokku and jaggery into boiling water and mixing well.

Tradition

Tokku is a pickled chutney found in every North Karnataka household. Variants of this chutney are also popular in Andhra Pradesh, always present amongst the pickles and dry chutneys at the centre of the table!

Tamarindus Indicus is native to the African Savannahs but has grown in India since pre-historic times. In 1298 Marco Polo referred to it as Tamarindi, a name that derives from the Arabic Tamarul-Hind, the date or fruit of India. Tamarind is used more widely in South India, especially to make rasam and even an amla+tamarind drink. Sorpotel, the pork dish from Goa, uses both vinegar and tamarind.

Health & Gourmet Tips

Tamarind is effective as a digestive, keeps away bacteria and is used as a remedy for bile disorders. An interesting variant of this chutney is Chigali, a sweet, hot and sour lollipop made by replacing green tamarind with the brown and dry ripe variety. It is mixed together with jaggery, chilli and jeera powder and pounded and shaped into a ball that is then mounted on a stick. It's the same combo that became popular in India as the button sized sweets that Jet Airways served to its passengers!

Kharda

Farmers' daily meal; adventure for city folk

Ingredients

1. Green chillies *125 gms*
2. Garlic *8-10 cloves*
3. Lime juice *1 tsp*
4. Fried methi seeds powdered *½ tsp*
5. Salt *to taste*
6. Tadka *(see below)*

Preparation

- Coarsely grind salt, green chillies and garlic. (This chutney tastes best when the chillies, garlic and salt
- are pounded in a mortar and pestle)
- Make tadka with 2 tsp of oil and ½ spoon of rai, add the ground chutney, add a tsp of lime juice and sauté the chutney for a few minutes
- Add the methi seed powder and mix well
- Store in an airtight container. This chutney is good for 8-10 days

Serving

Top off the kharda with some peanut oil and serve with bhakri.

Easy Variants

Kharda can also be mixed with yoghurt and a little besan to make a quick wet chutney.

Tradition

Kharda is eaten with bhakri at lunch in the searing afternoon heat, especially in the summer months. Farmers from Kolhapur, Solapur and Sangli in Maharashtra really relish this chutney.

Health & Gourmet Tips

Farmers carry this chutney to the fields along with bhakri and onions. The fiery chutney helps them sweat and get the matka (cooling) effect! The onion is a healthy accompaniment in the hot sun, absorbing all the heat.

The kharda mix could be used as a base mix for several dishes like a dry bhel. Adds zing to many Indian dishes! Use Kolhapuri Lavangi mirchis (from the Bird's eye chilli family) for the kharda to get a perfect strong flavour and pungency that will help beat the extreme heat of summer.

Kadley Baylay Chutney

The spicy protein salad

Ingredients
1. Channa dal *1 cup*
2. Green chillies *7-8*
3. Garlic *2-3 cloves*
4. Grated coconut *2 tbsp*
5. Coriander leaves *fistful*
6. Tamarind one *2 inch piece*
7. Salt *to taste*
8. Tadka *(see below)*

Preparation
- Soak channa dal in water for 2-3 hours,
- Soak tamarind in water for about 30 min
- Grind together coarsely channa dal, coconut, coriander, garlic, tamarind and salt
- Prepare tadka with 2 tsp oil, ½ tsp rai, a pinch of hing and 10-12 curry leaves and mix well with chutney before serving

Serving
This chutney goes well with dosas, uttappam, set dosas and pesarattu. It is also eaten with rice or chapattis in a traditional South Indian meal.

Easy Variants
This chutney is also made in its coarse and whole grain form where the soaked channa dal is ground lightly and mixed with the other ingredients. The tamarind can be replaced with grated green mango or lime juice for the sour taste.

Tradition
This is a traditional chutney used in festivals, weddings and religious ceremony meals in parts of South India. Kadley Baylay (channa dal in Kannada) is the main ingredient of this chutney. It is eaten as a pachadi or dal salad in these special meals.

Health & Gourmet Tips
Dals are an important source of proteins for vegetarians. They play a key role in rebuilding tissues and muscles. Whole moong sprouts tossed with lime juice, chillies, tomatoes and torn lettuce leaves make a great salad and are a tasty way to consume the healthy sprouts.

Onion Chutney

Disguise your onions and spice them up!

Ingredients

1. Onions *3 medium sized*
2. Chilli powder *2 tbsp*
3. Dry coconut *½ cup desiccated*
4. Tamarind extract *2 tbsp*
5. Jeera *½ tsp*
6. Tadka *(see below)*

Preparation

- Cut the onions into medium size pieces
- In a pan warm a little oil, add the red chilli powder, onions and salt
- Add cumin seeds and dry coconut and mix together
- Add the tamarind extract to the cut onions and blend this together in the chutney grinder
- Prepare tadka with 1 tsp oil, ½ tsp rai, a pinch of hing; and add to the chutney before serving.

Serving

Serve with wheat or jowar rotis or make sandwiches for teatime.

Easy Variants

The dry coconut may be replaced with wet coconut and the red chilli powder if replaced with fresh green chillies makes an interesting wet chutney. Add some coriander leaves for the fresh taste and colour.

Tradition

Onions are arguably the most used vegetable in the world. Onions and garlic come from the same family and are believed to have their origin around the region of Afghanistan. With its strong odour, tear jerking vapours and characteristic taste, it lends itself to creating a robust flavoured chutney.

Health & Gourmet Tips

Onions are known to have excellent stimulant, diuretic and expectorant qualities. The onion chutney goes with almost anything to add a 'punch' to any meal. For the chutney, use Reshampatta chillies for colour and heat or use Byadgi for a brilliant red colour but a milder flavour.

Fresh Coconut Chutney

Even better than the Udupi joints!

Ingredients

For green coconut chutney
1. Fresh coconut grated *2 cups*
2. Garlic *2 3 cloves*
3. Ginger *½ inch*
4. Coriander leaves *small bunch*
5. Green chillies *8-10*

For red coconut chutney
1. Fresh coconut grated *2 cups*
2. Dry red chillies *7-8 (soaked in warm water for 30 mins)*
3. Soaked channa dal *2 tbsp*
4. Ginger *½ inch*
5. Soaked tamarind *small lemon sized*

For white coconut chutney
1. Fresh grated coconut *2 cups*
2. Green Chillies *7-8*
3. Lime juice *1 tsp*
4. Salt *to taste*

Rai, urad dal, curry leaves, and oil for tadka

Preparation
- For any of the three chutneys mix together all the relevant ingredients, add salt to taste and grind coarsely.
- All three can be garnished with the tadka

Serving
These chutneys can be served with any South Indian snack idlis, dosas, vadas, upma, goond pangala or paniaram.

Easy Variants
Use fresh grated coconut, green chillies, a fistful of groundnuts soaked and deskinned and grind coarsely together. Garnish with tadka of oil, rai and hing.

Tradition
Coconut is a quintessential part of many Hindu rituals, especially in the coastal and southern parts of India. Indian mythology credits the creation of the coconut palm to the sage Vishwamitra, in order to prop up his friend Trishanku, who had been cast out from all the worlds by Indra for his misdeeds. The coconut palm evolved many million years ago and is believed to have its origins in Papua New Guinea. The word coco in Spanish and macoco in Portuguese mean monkey's face - describing how a large coconut looks.

Freshly grated coconut or coconut milk are the base of cooking in coastal Karnataka and Maharashtra and other parts of the west coast of India. The coconut chutney is synonymous with South Indian snacks and has been taken to all parts of the country by the ubiquitous Udipi restaurants.

Health & Gourmet Tips
Tender coconut water is sold at most street corners in South India and outside hospitals, prescribed as a drink that nurses patients back to the pink of health. Coconut is highly nutritious and rich in fibre, vitamins, and minerals. It is classified as a 'functional food' because it provides many health benefits beyond its nutritional content. Coconut oil is of special interest because it possesses healing properties far beyond that of any other dietary oil and is extensively used in traditional medicine among Asian and Pacific populations.

Coconut chutneys are best made in a rubba (or the modern day rubba - the wet grinder), a stone mortar and pestle, that grinds the ingredients together, while still retaining the texture of the grated coconut.

Amsol Chutney

Tangy...and that rich purple-pink

Ingredients
1. Amsol *10-15*
2. Dry coconut grated *2 tbsp*
3. Methi seeds *½ tbsp*
4. Hing *½ tsp*
5. Jaggery *lump size of a medium lemon*
6. Green chillies *4-5*
7. Salt *to taste*

Preparation
- Soak amsol in water for 3-4 hours
- Roast methi seeds in a little oil, set aside
- Grind together amsol, dry coconut, hing, methi seeds, jaggery and salt
- This chutney tastes best when pounded in a mortar and pestle. Start with amsol and salt, pound it to a coarse texture
- Add coconut and hing and pound
- Add jaggery and green chillies and pound to a smooth paste

Serving
Serve this as a relish or pickle to be eaten with rice dishes or chapattis, much like a mango chutney.

Easy Variants
Try a similar chutney with tamarind.
Take a lump of amsol chutney and add it to coconut milk, chill and savour the cool drink popularly called Solkadi. Amsol is also used in Maharashtrian and Gujarati cuisine as a souring agent much like lime juice or amchur.

Tradition
Amsol, Kokam or Mangosteen, is a prune-like very sour fruit that is pitted and dried for table use. Amsol is used extensively in cuisine from the West Coast of India, much like tamarind is used in South India. Mangosteen is an important ingredient in Malay cuisine.

This chutney is often made amongst west coast Brahmin families for *shraadha* ceremonies, in memory of the dead - and some hesitate to make it on happy occasions. But hey, that's history!

Health & Gourmet Tips
Eat amsol chutney or drink solkadi as a coolant during the summer months. A great acidity buster, it's also a good digestive aid that gets your juices flowing.

Apricot Chutney

British Raj nostalgia

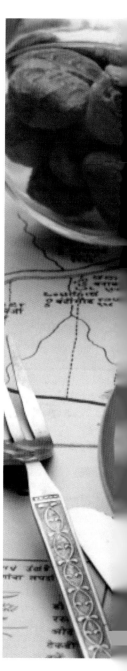

Ingredients

1. Dried apricots *250 gm*
2. Cinnamon powder *1 pinch*
3. Dry sherry *¼ cup*
4. Cardamom powder *1 pinch*
5. Brown sugar *½ cup*
6. Raisins *¼ cup*
7. Red chilli flakes *1 tsp*
8. Lemon juice *2 tbsp*
9. Almond extract *1 drop*
10. Water *1 cup*
11. Pinch of salt

Preparation

- Soak apricots in water for 4 hours
- Boil 1 cup water
- Drop the apricots in the boiling water for a few minutes, drain
- Chop fine
- Combine all ingredients together in a heavy bottomed saucepan and bring to a boil, reduce heat, let simmer
- Stir frequently till the mixture thickens

Serving

This is typically served with sausages, pork chops, ribs and steak. Serve it as a tangy jam on toasted bread.

Easy Variants

The British created many fruit based chutneys. Try this recipe with strawberries, raspberries, mango or apple.

Tradition

A gift of the British during colonial times several fruit based relishes and chutneys were cooked up. Several of these were even exported back to England as brand name recipes - Colonel Skinner's, Major Grey's and Bengal Club chutney.

Health & Gourmet Tips

Like many sweet fruits, dried apricots are classed as 'cold' foods in Ayurvedic terms, and have an alkaline reaction in the body.

Green Mango Chutney

Know the five tastes; evoke childhood memories

Ingredients

1. Green mangoes *2 medium sized*
2. Red chilli powder *8 tbsp*
3. Dry coconut *1 cup grated*
4. Jaggery *1 cup sliced*
5. Methi seeds *1 tsp*
6. Rai *1 tsp*
7. Turmeric powder *¼ tsp*
8. Hing *½ tsp*
9. Urad dal *½ tsp*
10. Channa dal *½ tsp*
11. Salt *to taste*
12. Tadka *(see below)*

Preparation

- Dry roast methi seeds, set aside
- In a little oil, roast urad dal and channa dal till they turn golden brown, set aside
- Peel the green mangoes with a peeler; grate the mangoes and discard seed
- In a chutney grinder coarsely grind the methi seeds, urad dal and channa dal
- Mix grated mango, grated coconut, red chilli powder, salt and blend, add jaggery and blend together
- Prepare tadka with 3 tbsp oil, ½ tsp rai, a pinch of hing, and turmeric powder; garnish chutney with this tadka

Serving

Serve with wheat or jowar roti. This chutney goes well with brown bread or pita bread or as a dip with chips.

Easy Variants

This chutney can also be made using fresh grated coconut. Replace dry coconut with ½ cup of wet coconut and follow the same steps. Chutney made with dry coconut can be stored for 4-5 days without refrigeration. The British colonial style mango chutney or relish is another popular variant of the mango chutney, like the apricot chutney.

Tradition

Mango chutney contains all the five rasas or tastes sour (green mango), bitter (methi), pungent (chillies), sweet (jaggery) and salty (salt). This is a popular chutney in the southern and western parts of India and is made in every household during the summer. Mango is a big part of India's culture - its religious texts, sculptures and handicrafts. Buddha rested and preached in a mango grove donated by one of his followers. The hills of Northeastern India, bordering Myanmar, are believed to be the origin of the mango; wild varieties still grow there in the forests. The Mughals and the Portuguese created many varieties of the mango by grafting that are cultivated even today - Langda, Dussehri, Chowsa, Ratnal, Pairi, Banganpalli, Neelam and Alphonso.

Health & Gourmet Tips

A great chutney for the hot Indian summer. Try this chutney with different varieties of mangoes and in different stages of tartness. For the best flavour and colour for this chutney use Byadgi chilli powder. Have this chutney with the other summer goodies, and round it off with a refreshing mango panna (drink made from cooked green mango pulp).

Green Apple Chutney

Pluck it early - spice up the fruit from the cold places

Ingredients

1. Green apple seeded, cored and diced *1 large*
2. Raisins *2 tbsp*
3. Onion *¼ cup chopped*
4. Sugar *¼ cup*
5. White vinegar or cider vinegar *2 tbsp*
6. Rai *2 tsp*
7. Sugar *1 tsp*
8. Red pepper flakes *¼ tsp*
9. Canola or sunflower oil *1 tbsp*
10. Salt *to taste*

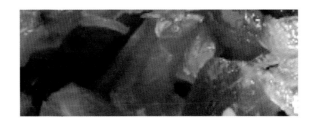

Preparation

- Heat the oil, add onions and sauté till softened
- Add sugar and vinegar and cook until sugar dissolves and makes syrup
- While the liquid is hot, stir in the diced apple and remaining ingredients and stir together

Serving

This is a popular fruit chutney/relish served with pork chops, barbecued chicken and lamb.

Easy Variants

Replace the apple with other fruits - pears, plums, guavas or berries - and cook them into spicy marmalades and relishes. Take away the onions from the ingredients; add a pinch of cinnamon powder to give it some more flavour. Eat it spread over freshly baked bread and have your very own spicy 'apple pie'.

Tradition

A contemporary chutney or relish that blends the fruit from the cold places with the spices of the warm east.

Health & Gourmet Tips

Apples are a great source of antioxidants, iron and fibre. An apple a day keeps the doctor way, goes the old adage!

Pineapple Chutney

Babu Moshai ! Spice up the big, rough apple

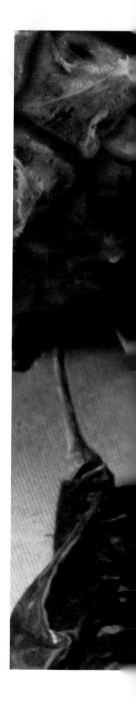

Ingredients
1. Pineapple peeled and diced
   (with the 'eyes' removed) *1 cup*
2. Turmeric powder *½ tsp*
3. Red chilli powder *½ tbsp*
4. Water *2 tbsp*
5. Curry leaves *4-5*
6. Jaggery or palm sugar or date jaggery *1-2 tbsp*
7. Grind to a paste the following:
   Coconut *2 tbsp*
   Dry red chillies *4*
   Rai *½ tsp*
   Methi seeds *½ tsp*
   Jeera *½ tsp*

Preparation
- Pour pineapple, salt, water, and turmeric, curry leaves and chilli powder in a saucepan.
- Bring to a boil, reduce the heat and cook for 15 minutes
- Add jaggery; as the jaggery melts add the ground paste
- Continue sautéing till the water evaporates

Serving
This is a typical Bengali chutney served with khichadi especially during the festivities of Durga Puja.

Easy Variants
Add garlic, dates, cardamom and vinegar to create a pineapple chutney with additional flavours and tastes.

Tradition
The development of the pineapple is attributed to the Indians of the lowlands of South America. First discovered by Columbus, on his second voyage to an island he called Guadeloupe. The word pineapple derives from the large stone pine of southern Europe that it resembles.

In most Indian languages it is called ananas. By Akbar's time it was being extensively grown even around Agra. By 1665 the 'innumerable islands of Bengal abounded with fruit trees and pineapples'. Pineapples continue to be a popular fruit in Bengal and the northeast and pineapple chutney is one of the signature relishes of this region.

Health & Gourmet Tips
A good source of vitamin C. It offers your body excellent protection against free radicals, the substances that attack healthy cells. Fresh pineapple is full of sulphur, containing protein-digesting compounds.

Date and Tamarind Chutney

Lip smacking must for those chatpata chaats!

Ingredients

1. Seedless dates *100 gms*
2. Jaggery crumbled *1 cup*
3. Extract of tamarind *½ cup*
   (to extract tamarind soak lime sized lump in water for about 30 minutes, extract pulp)
4. Chilli powder *2 tsp*
5. Rock salt *1 tbsp*
6. Black peppercorns *1 tsp*
7. Salt *to taste*

Preparation

- Wash the dates and soak in water for half an hour
- Soak tamarind in water for half an hour
- Boil tamarind extract and dates together for about 15 min
- Strain this extract using a fine strainer
- Add 2 cups of water and the jaggery
- Boil the whole mixture till it comes to a ketchup consistency
- Add chilli powder, salt, rock salt and coarsely ground black peppercorns

Serving

The most popular use of this chutney is in chaats and bhelpuri. It is also served with samosas and batata wadas and to garnish dahi wadas and kachori.

Easy Variants

Add dhania and jeera powder to add spice and body to this chutney.

Tradition

Tamarind 'Tamarindus indicus' has been a big part of South Indian cuisine for many centuries. Called Puli in Tamil, it later became the generic word for sourness.

In the northern and western states of India, tamarind is used mainly to prepare chutney and the sourness is balanced off with sweet from jaggery and dates.

Health & Gourmet Tips

Tamarind is effective as a digestive, keeps away bacteria and is used as a remedy for bile disorders. Dates are a rich source of iron and in Ayurveda it is believed that dates keep the inner body warm.

Walnut Chutney

The nutty one from Paradise

Ingredients

1. Walnuts *8-10*
2. Curd *½ cup*
3. Kashmiri red chilli powder *2 tsp*
4. Water
5. Salt *to taste*

Preparation

- Crack open the walnuts and grind together with salt and chilli powder *(Try this - take two walnuts with their shells and press together on the seams; the walnuts will crack open)*
- Mix yoghurt and a little water
- Mix well until it has a viscous consistency

Serving

This Kashmiri chetin (chutney) is very good in a plain butter sandwich, as also with any Kashmiri or North West Frontier region meal.

Easy Variants

The Kashmiri pudina chetin is also made with fresh pudina (mint) and walnuts. Dried crushed mint can also be used to make this chutney. Dried mint is good to have at hand during winter.
Pistachios and pine nuts make good substitutes for walnuts.

Tradition

Doon Chetin is a popular chutney from Kashmir, served at Kashmiri weddings. An important part of the grand Waazwaan conjured up by the Vasta Waza (the head chef) served with his other specialities.

Health & Gourmet Tips

Try this chetin as a dip with fresh-from-the-garden celery, carrot or beet root sticks. Walnuts are one of the best plant sources of protein. They are rich in fibre, vitamin B, magnesium, and antioxidants such as vitamin E. Walnuts have been shown to lower LDL cholesterol. Walnuts have significantly high amounts of omega 3 fatty acids.

Brinjal Chutney

Love it or hate it, but do try it!

Ingredients

1. Brinjal *1 medium sized*
2. Green chillies *3-4*
3. Garlic *3 cloves*
4. Coriander *few sprigs*
5. Salt *to taste*

Preparation

- Apply a thin coat of oil on the brinjal, the green chillies and the garlic
- Roast them on direct flame, at medium heat
- Cover and let cool to room temperature
- Peel the roasted brinjal
- Mash the brinjal with a fork
- Mash the green chillies and the garlic
- Add salt and chopped coriander and mix well together

Serving

Traditionally this chutney is eaten with jowar bhakri, chapatti or rice. Try this chutney with pita bread, chips or with bread sticks - a spicy takeoff on the Middle Eastern favourite Baba Ghanouj.

Easy Variants

A couple of teaspoons of roasted til or groundnut powder add a nutty flavour and texture to this chutney.

Tradition

Known throughout the world by different names - egg plant, aubergine and brinjal, this vegetable has a cult following. Many dislike the vegetable, but those who like it, are real devotees! The best known dish in India is perhaps roasted brinjal - baingan bharta, the dhaba classic.

Health & Gourmet Tips

Cut this vegetable into thin slices, marinate it with chilli powder and spices and shallow fry for spicy brinjal 'chips'. Our favourite is stuffed brinjal - cut slits, stuff it with your favourite spices, nuts, vegetables, and steam or shallow fry. Vangi bhaat is a favourite rice dish in Tamil Nadu.

Cabbage Chutney

Pack those layers with chilli - the spicy coleslaw

Ingredients
1. Cabbage *250 gms*
2. Green chillies *7-8*
3. Urad dal *2 tsp*
4. Coriander leaves *a few*
5. Lime juice *1 tsp*
6. For tadka - oil, rai, curry leaves, hing
7. Salt *to taste*

Preparation
- Wash and cut the cabbage coarsely
- Chop the green chillies
- Dry roast the urad dal and set aside to cool
- Prepare tadka with oil, rai, curry leaves and hing
- Add the chopped green chillies to the tadka
- Add the chopped cabbage
- Saute and cover with a lid and let the cabbage cook; this will take about 5-10 mins
- Let cool
- In a blender coarsely grind, the urad dal, the cooked cabbage and the coriander leaves, add a dash of lime juice and salt to taste and blend together once again

Serving
This chutney goes well with chapattis, rice and toasted bread.

Easy Variants
Add little bit of tamarind pulp to the cabbage chutney to make a sour and spicy version.

Tradition
The botanical name for cabbage is Brassica oleracea capitata. The English name 'cabbage' comes from the French caboche, meaning head, referring to its round form.

Cabbage has been domesticated for over 2,500 years. North China is probably the original home of the cabbage. The ancient Chinese considered it a 'cooling' food in the yin and yang construct. Cabbage is favoured for pickling and is considered ts'ai or suitable to go with rice. Although cabbage is often connected to the Irish, the Celts took cabbage to Europe from Asia around 600 B.C. Since cabbage grows well in cool climates, yields large harvests, and stores well during winter, it soon became a major crop in Europe.

Pickled cabbage known as kimchee is a staple throughout Korea. Germans love their sauerkraut and the Dutch their coleslaw.

Cabbage and cauliflower came to India post 1850, for use by the British. Like many other vegetables it soon spread to all parts of India. This chutney is a popular pachadi in Andhra Pradesh.

Health & Gourmet Tips
Eat this chutney with plain rice and hot ghee - Andhra style. Try spicy variants of kimchee, coleslaw and sauerkraut.

Cabbage is a rich source of vitamin C, fibre, iron, calcium and potassium. The odour that it emits comes from the sulphur content of cabbage which helps the body resist bacteria and protects the protoplasm of the cells.

Radish Chutney

No horses; just the radish

Ingredients
1. White radish *3*
2. Chilli powder *3 tbsp*
3. Grated wet coconut *1 tbsp*
4. A little tamarind or lime juice
5. Salt *to taste*

Preparation
- Grate the radish and set aside in a plate at an angle, drain out any excess water/juice
- Blend all the ingredients in a chutney mixer
- Garnish with tadka of oil, rai and hing

Serving
Serve with chapatti, rice or bhakri. Good as part of a veg sandwich too.

Easy Variants
Instead of white radish you can use red radish, serve with tostitos, chips and hard bread.

Tradition
The radish is a very ancient plant, believed to have been developed in the Fertile Crescent of domestication. The radish in India is long, white and conical shaped. The ones in Europe are typically red, white, purple and globular in form. Radishes are a big part of Kashmiri cuisine, where they are grown in floating gardens of water weeds bound by mud from the lake. Radish is also made into a sabzi cooked along with its leaves.

Health & Gourmet Tips
Radish cools the body, especially in summer. Radish juice is prescribed for controlling fever. Rich in vitamin C & A, radish has cancer protective properties and helps maintain a healthy gall bladder and liver.

Red Pumpkin Peel Chutney

Not just for Halloween

Ingredients

1. Pumpkin peel *of ½ kg red pumpkin*
2. Dry red chillies *8-10*
3. Urad dal *2 tbsp*
4. Channa dal *1 tbsp*
5. Til *1½ tbsp*
6. Curry leaves *4-5*
7. Tamarind *size of a small lemon*
8. Jaggery *as much as the tamarind*
9. Tadka *(see below)*
10. Salt *to taste*

Preparation

- Finely chop the red pumpkin peel
- Dry roast the til on medium flame till golden brown or till they splutter
- Roast channa dal and urad dal on medium heat till golden brown
- Roast red chillies
- Set all the four roasted items aside to cool
- In a small kadhai, make tadka with 2 tbsp oil, ½ spoon rai, pinch of hing and a fistful of curry leaves
- Add chopped red pumpkin peel, add salt after the peel is soft and cooked
- Let cool and grind together with til, channa dal, urad dal, red chillies, tamarind and jaggery.

Serving

This chutney can be served with chapatti or jowar bhakri. Try it with a muffin, a bagel, a croissant or a bread bun.

Easy Variants

The ridge gourd peel chutney, covered separately in this book, is another interesting use of the peel of the gourd family. Try making pumpkin salsa or chutney at your next Halloween party!

Tradition

Pumpkins are a part of the gourd family that includes melons (watermelon, muskmelon), snake gourd (parwal), ridge gourd (dodka), bottle gourd (dudhi), bitter gourd (karela) and cucumber (khira). All these gourds are a major part of Indian cuisine in different parts of the country. Gourds are indigenous to India and Africa and have been traditionally grown along river banks in the summer months. Gourds are used to make sabzis, cooked with dal, and made into sweets and halwas (petha).

Pumpkins come in many shapes, sizes and colours - round, oblong, small, large, ridged, smooth, yellow and orange. Pumpkins are believed to have come to India from the New World (America) via Africa, floating on the high seas! Called kaddu, kumbalkayi and several other names in India, the red pumpkin is used to make sabzis, dry or wet curries, and in sambar; even its peel is used to make this interesting chutney.

Health & Gourmet Tips

Bottle gourd or dudhi juice has become a big fad in India, sold early mornings outside most parks as the medicine for hypertension. Almost all parts of the pumpkin are edible. Pumpkin seeds are dried and eaten and are very good source of quality nutrition and vitamin E. Potassium in the pumpkin aids in balancing fluid levels in the body, helps in energy production and controlling blood pressure.

Ridge Gourd Chutney

Don't discard those peels and ridges!

Ingredients

1. Ridges *of 4 ridge gourds*
2. Green chillies *5-6*
3. Urad dal *1 tbsp*
4. Oil *2 tsp*
5. Rai *½ tsp*
6. Hing *½ tsp*
7. Salt *to taste*

Preparation

- Peel the ridges with a peeler
- Cut the green chillies into big pieces
- Prepare tadka with oil, rai and hing
- Add the green chillies and sauté for a minute
- Add the ridge peels and sauté and cook with lid till tender, set aside to cool
- Dry roast urad dal on medium heat till golden brown
- Powder the urad dal in a blender and add the cooked chillies and peels
- Add salt and blend together coarsely

Serving

Can be served with chapatti, rice or bhakri.

Easy Variants

This chutney can be made using either urad dal, peanuts or sesame seeds. Add a little tamarind extract and a small piece of jaggery while blending.

Tradition

Ridge gourd is one of the many gourds found in India. The ridge gourd sabzis are traditionally prepared along with urad or moong dal, sauted together with oil and masala.

Health & Gourmet Tips

This is an interesting chutney, in which the ridges and peels of the gourd which would have been otherwise discarded, are put to great use. The ridges are a rich source of fibre and iron.

Green Peas Chutney

Our dad's favourite quick-fix chutney

Ingredients

1. Fresh shelled green peas *1 cup*
2. Green chillies *5-6*
3. Shredded coconut *1 tbsp*
4. Tadka with oil, rai and curry leaves
5. Lime juice
6. Salt *to taste*

Preparation

- Grind together coarsely shelled peas, coconut and green chillies
- Prepare tadka and mix well with a dash of lime juice

Serving

Can be served with chapatti, or as a salsa dip with chips.

Easy Variants

Make this chutney as a healthy, spicy salad, without the shredded coconut. Serve this salad tossed with fresh and crisp lettuce or methi leaves and fresh tomato cut into small cubes.

Tradition

Peas have been used as food since ancient times and were domesticated in the area of the Fertile Crescent as early as in 7000 BC. In India, green peas are cooked as a vegetable, or along with rice (peas pulao), made into a soup, or used as paratha filling in North India.

Health & Gourmet Tips

Peas are a cold, dry and sweet food according to Ayurveda. Peas kabab is a great equivalent of the meat kababs for vegetarians. Mash the shelled peas lightly, mix with other ingredients of the chutney and add channa dal or corn starch to the mixture. Shape the mixture into small 2" discs. Steam these pieces or shallow/deep fry and serve hot with spicy coriander chutney.

Vadmurk - Roasted Capsicum Chutney

Fiery in more ways than one!

Ingredients
1. Green capsicums *3*
2. Green chillies *3-4*
3. Garlic *2 cloves*
4. Yoghurt *1 cup*
5. Salt *to taste*
6. Tadka *(see below)*

Preparation
- Smear the capsicums with a thin layer of oil and roast them directly on the flame, on medium heat
- Similarly roast the green chillies and garlic
- With a fork, mash the green chillies, garlic and green capsicum. Beat the yoghurt lightly and mix
- Add salt and mix well
- Prepare tadka with 1 tbsp oil, ½ tsp rai, ½ tsp urad dal, pinch of hing, and garnish the chutney.

Serving
This is an excellent chutney/raita with chapattis and jowar bhakris.

Easy Variants
To the roasted capsicum, add 1 cup of phutanay dal and sauté along with green chillies. Season with tadka, cool and serve this as a dry variant of this chutney.

Tradition
Capsicum, the sweet 'bell pepper', the mother of the chilli, is the most famous export of the New World to Asia. Not as pungent as its thinner cousins, it makes an excellent roasted salad and sabzi.

Health & Gourmet Tips
Roasting capsicum on burning coal embers (rather than on a gas flame) smokes it and gives it an earthy flavour. Stuffed capsicum sabzi is an all-time favourite of capsicum connoisseurs.

Capsicum comes with all the health benefits of chillies, beneficial to the mucous membranes, eyes and skin, helps ward off infections, promotes cardiovascular health, by helping lower blood pressure and has antioxidant properties that neutralise the free radicals responsible for damaging tissue and cells.

Chilli Platter

Fire up your card session in the rains

Ingredients

Chilli Bhajjis

1. Chillies *12-15*
2. Jeera powder *2 tsp*
3. Salt for chillies *to taste*
4. Besan *1 cup*
5. Salt for besan batter *to taste*
6. Pinch of baking soda
7. Oil for deep frying *1 cup*

Stuffed Mirchi

1. Big long chillies (Panvel, Bhavnagari chilli or Banana peppers or Serrano peppers) *6-8*
2. Besan *2 cups*
3. Saunf powder *3 tsp*
(Slightly roast the saunf and grind into a powder)
4. Chilli powder *1 tbsp*
5. Dhania powder *1 tsp*
6. Jeera powder *1 tsp*
7. Coriander leaves *a few*
8. Oil for shallow frying *3 tbsp*
9. Lime juice *2 tsp*
10. Salt *to taste*

Menasinakai Balaka (Sun dried spiced chillies)

1. Chillies *10-12*
2. Methi seeds *1 tsp*
3. Hing *a pinch*
4. Sour curd *1/4 cup*
5. Salt *to taste*

Preparation

Chilli Bhajjis

- Wash and pat dry the chillies
- Slit the chillies lengthwise, keeping the stalk on
- Smear the cut edge with salt and jeera powder and set aside
- In a bowl mix besan with salt and a pinch of baking soda and mix to make a thick batter
- In a deep frying dish heat oil
- Dip each slit chilli in the besan batter and carefully release in the hot oil; deep fry on medium heat till golden brown, drain oil and remove from oil
- Serve hot

Stuffed Mirchi

- Wash the big long chillies and pat dry
- Slit the chillies lengthwise and remove the membrane and the seeds
- In a mixing bowl mix together besan, saunf powder, dhania powder, jeera powder, red chilli powder, salt and lime juice.
- If required, add a few drops of water to make into a semi dry mixture
- Divide the stuffing into 6-8 parts (enough for each chilli)
- Fill each chilli with the stuffing, press the stuffing gently into the chilli and press the slit shut
- In a shallow pan heat oil on medium heat, drop each stuffed chilli into the pan, sear each side and keep turning till the chillies are cooked
- Serve hot

- **Mensinakai Balaka** (Sun dried spiced chillies)
  These chillies can be stored for over a year if stored
  in an airtight container. Summer is the best time to
  make them as the sun will dry them thoroughly.
- Wash and pat dry the chillies
- Dry roast the methi seeds and grind into a powder
- Slit the chillies lengthwise, leaving the stalk on
- Smear the inside of the chillies with salt and methi
  powder
- Lightly beat the curd and pour over the chillies, mix
  lightly and make sure all the chillies are evenly
  coated with the beaten curd
- Sun dry these chillies thoroughly, it will take 2- 3
  sunny days to dry these chillies; make sure to
  bring the chillies into the house in the evenings
- Store in an airtight container
- For serving, the chillies can be shallow or deep fried

Serving
Chilli bhajjis are eaten as a snack, with a hot cup of
chai.
Stuffed mirchi makes a colourful and feisty side-serve to
any Indian meal.
Mensinakai balaka is fried as a part of the tadka or
seasoning and used to spice up curd-rice.

Easy Variants
Barbecue the stuffed chillies for a subtle smoky
flavour.

Tradition
Most Indians are bhajji addicts. It is the favourite
accompaniment to a game of cards and gambling
sessions along with a hot cup of chai, particularly
in the monsoons. Bhajjis are made from almost any
vegetable, chilli bhajjis being the most rustic and
'macho' amongst them all! Bhajjis have been
around in the Indian subcontinent for many
centuries, evidently having influenced the popular
Japanese snack, tempura, when the concept of the
fish bhajji was taken to Japan by Catholic
Portuguese missionaries.

The stuffed and dried chillies are a popular chilli
accompaniment with curd-rice in most parts of
South India. The stuffed chilli in various forms,
including stuffed capsicum, is made both as a snack
and a side dish or sabzi. The stuffed chilli is either
fried, cooked or steamed.

Health & Gourmet Tips
These chilli preparations retain the goodness of the
chilli and all its healthy properties.

Tomato Salsa

The American favourite

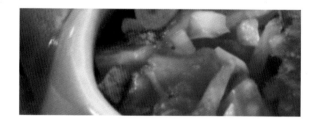

Ingredients

1. Onions (finely chopped) *3 tbsp*
2. Garlic (minced) *2 small cloves*
3. Ripe red tomatoes *3 large (about 250 gms)
   (peeled, seeds removed, and chopped into bite size
   pieces)*
4. Hot chile peppers *2 (serrano or habanero) finely
   chopped. (Remove the membrane and the seeds if you
   want to reduce the heat)*
5. Minced coriander *2-3 tbsp*
6. Lime juice *1 ½ -2 tbsp*
7. Salt and pepper *to taste*

Preparation

- Put chopped onion and garlic in a strainer; pour 2
  cups of boiling water over them, let drain
  thoroughly. Discard water. Cool
- Combine onions and garlic with chopped tomatoes,
  peppers, coriander, lime juice, salt and pepper.
  Refrigerate for 2 to 4 hours to blend flavours

Serving

Garnish with a few leaves of flat leaf parsley. Serve
with tostitos, tortillas and chicken. Cut up some toasted
bread and serve with salsa. Warm up some corn
tortillas, smear with salsa, add avocado, lettuce and
thinly sliced onion, top with cheese and serve.

Easy Variants

Substitute the ripe red tomatoes with green unripe
tomatoes for a green tomato salsa.

Tradition

Salsas are synonymous with Mexican cuisine. The
salsa can be traced to the Aztecs, Mayans and Incas.
The Spaniards first encountered tomatoes after their
conquest of Mexico in 1519-1521, which marked
the beginning of the Tomato Salsa sauce. Aztec
lords combined tomatoes with chile peppers, ground
squash seeds and consumed them mainly as a
condiment served with turkey, venison, lobster, and
fish. This combination was subsequently called
Salsa!

Health & Gourmet Tips

Tomatoes, which are actually a fruit and not a
vegetable, are loaded with all kinds of health
benefits for the body. High levels of lycopene, that
is an important element of tomatoes, are known to
stave off prostrate, cervical, colon and rectal
cancers; as well as cancers of the stomach, mouth,
pharynx and esophagus.

Corn Salsa

Gifts from Mexico

Ingredients
1. Corn kernels *2 cups*
2. Orange bell pepper *1*
3. Red bell pepper *1*
4. Green bell pepper *1*
5. Lime juice *2 tbsp*
6. Salt and pepper *to taste*

Preparation
- Boil the corn kernels till tender
- Set aside to cool
- Chop the bell peppers, remove the seeds and the membrane and cut into small pieces.
- Mix together the corn, chopped bell peppers, salt, pepper and lime juice

Serving
This salsa can be served as a salad or salsa along with some tortilla chips and nachos.

Easy Variants
Roast 3 corns on the cob. Remove the kernels and follow the same procedure. To add a little pungency, mix in two finely chopped jalapenos.

Tradition
Corn and chiles are perhaps the best-known Mexican gifts to mankind. Both gifts have travelled far and wide over the centuries and influenced many cuisines. If you could pick a single food that exemplifies the Americas - no food really screams 'American' like corn. It is the largest crop in the U.S. in terms of production. It has regularly graced dinner tables, including Thanksgiving dinners, from the 1600s.

Small towns all around America's heartland hold corn festivals. In Iowa, the nation's #1 corn producer, about half the farming land is devoted exclusively to corn!

Corn is native to the Americas. The Native Americans grew it thousands of years before Christopher Columbus arrived in the New World. Petrified cobs that are thousands of years old have been discovered and are evidence of the presence of corn since ancient days.

Health & Gourmet Tips
Corn Clubs and dishes made from corn have proliferated all over the world. Several neo-Indian dishes such as corn 'pattice', corn bhel, corn chips and the ever popular popcorn, is now available in all parts of the country.

The high amount of fibre present in corn helps lower cholesterol levels and also reduces the risk of colon cancer. Consumed in moderate quantities, it has been seen to be beneficial for those suffering from diabetes. Owing to the presence of thiamin, corn has been said to help in the metabolism of carbohydrates. The insoluble fibre in corn makes it good for those suffering from common digestive ailments, like constipation and hemorrhoids.

Thai Red Curry Paste

Your trip to Bangkok

Ingredients

1. Small Thai red dry chillies *13-15*
(deseeded and soaked in water for about 30 min)
2. Chopped onions *3 tbsp*
3. Chopped garlic *4 tbsp*
4. Galangal (Thai ginger) *1 tbsp*
5. Lemon grass *2 tbsp chopped*
6. Kaffir lime rind *2 tsp*
(or substitute with fresh lime peel)
7. Coriander root *1 tbsp*
8. White peppercorns *1 tbsp*
9. Ground roasted cumin seeds *½ tsp*
10. Sea salt *1 tsp*
11. Fish sauce *1 tsp*
(Vegetarians replace with 2 tsp soy sauce)
12. Shrimp sauce *1 tsp*
(Vegetarians may omit this)

Preparation

- Pound all the ingredients together in a mortar and pestle or blend together in an electric blender
- If you use an electric blender you may need to add about 1 tbsp of water

Serving

This curry paste can be used to prepare vegetable curry, chicken curry or seafood curry.

Easy Variants

The Green curry paste can be made using the same procedure and ingredients, only replace the red chillies with about 7-8 small hot green chillies. Add this paste to boiled noodles, sautéed vegetables and garnish with peanuts to make pad thai.

Tradition

Thai curry paste is the identity of Thai food. Green or red curry paste is the core flavouring for a number of Thai dishes. A traditional Thai curry is made with a subtle blend of hot, salty, sweet and sour flavours to get the taste buds tingling.

Health & Gourmet Tips

The blend of numerous herbs and spices makes the Thai curry paste a complex potion by itself. Galangal is a source of sodium, iron, vitamins A and C. Lemon grass is known for its calming effect that relieves insomnia or stress. It also has antibacterial and antifungal properties. Mixed with pepper, it's a home therapy for menstrual troubles and nausea. Consumed as tea, it is an effective diuretic. Kafir lime is a good source of vitamin C.

Harissa & Piri Piri

Gifts from the wild continent

Ingredients

Harissa
1. Dry red chillies *10 to 12*
2. Ground coriander seeds *1 tsp*
3. Ground cumin seeds *1 tsp*
4. Ground caraway seeds *1 tsp*
5. Garlic *3 cloves minced*
6. Olive oil *2 tbsp*
7. Salt *to taste*

Piri Piri
1. Dry red hot chillies *10*
2. Lemon juice *½ cup fresh*
3. Cilantro *2 tbsp finely chopped or dry*
4. Parsley *1 tbsp chopped or dry*
5. Garlic *5 cloves chopped*
6. Olive oil *½ cup*
7. Turmeric powder *1 tsp*
8. Salt *to taste*

Preparation

Harissa
- Soak the dried red chillies in hot water for 30 mins
- Drain, remove stems and seeds
- In a food processor, combine chillies, garlic, salt and olive oil
- Blend the remaining spices into a smooth paste

Piri piri
- Roughly chop the chillies, cover with boiling water and soak for one hour
- Drain the water and in a blender drop all the ingredients with the soaked chillies, except the olive oil. Blend together adding the olive oil as you blend.

Serving
Store in an airtight container. Drizzle a small amount of olive oil on top to keep fresh. Can be stored in the refrigerator for a month. It is traditionally served with couscous but can be used as a flavouring in soups, salads and can be served as a dip with bread.

Easy Variants
The Yemeni seasoning known as zhug is similar to harissa, and is made by adding half a teaspoon each

Tradition
Harissa and Piri Piri are popular chilli sauces of Africa - Harissa in North Africa stretching right up to Arabia, and Piri Piri in South Africa. Piri Piri, named after the Swahili word for chillies, is a chilli sauce that has been popularised by its packaged equivalents and the South African chain Nando's and their Piri Piri Chicken. Harissa is a hot chilli sauce from Morocco, Algeria and Tunisia. Used as a meat or aubergine rub and as a flavouring for couscous, it is available extensively in its commercial bottled form.

Health & Gourmet Tips
A Tunisian blend, tabil, is made in the same way as Harissa except it contains hotter chillies and no cumin, making it relatively hotter. Traditionally, harissa is used commonly as a sauce in a small dish in the same way that sauce appears on the table in South East Asian cuisine. It is also used now in cold meat sandwiches as a spicy alternative to mustard. Harissa is delicious on crusty bread that has been spread with hummus.

Chinese Dips

The Chinese colours - firing up GDP rates

Ingredients

For all the three dips:

1. Red chillies *20 g*
2. Green chillies *20 g*
3. Chilli flakes *3 tbsp*
4. Garlic *4-5 cloves*
5. White vinegar *1 cup*
6. Soya sauce *1 cup*
7. Sesame oil *¼ cup*
8. Vegetable oil *½ cup*
9. Salt *to taste*

Preparation

- These dips are quick and easy to prepare.
- For dip 1 mix the sesame oil and the vegetable oil with the chilli flakes and finely chopped garlic
- For dip 2 mix soya sauce with the finely chopped red chillies
- For dip 3 mix vinegar with the finely chopped green chillies

Serving

Popular appetizers like spring rolls and egg rolls just wouldn't taste the same without a flavourful dipping sauce. Dim sums and momos are served with these dips.

Easy Variants

Try the dip with fermented black beans. Chinese fermented black beans (doubanjiang, also called salted black beans) are made by fermenting soybeans in garlic, salt and other spices.

Tradition

These dips are synonymous with Chinese and Thai cuisine. The Chinese, especially in the Sichuan and Hunan regions, adopted the chilli into their cuisine after Portuguese traders introduced it. It was quickly paired with other Chinese base ingredients - sesame oil, soya sauce and rice vinegar.

Health & Gourmet Tips

The fiery chillies come with all their well-known antioxidants and other health benefits. Sesame oil is known for its preservative qualities and extensively used in pickles. Vinegar made from fermented rice, grapes or sugarcane has a special place in several cuisines - used to great effect in Goan vindaloo, sorpotel and prawn balchao.

Glossary

badalphul	star anise
badi elaichi	black cardamom
besan	gram flour
channa dal	split gram
dagadphul	a variety of lichen (not to be confused with star anise)
dalchini	cinnamon
dhania	corriander
elaichi/velchi	cardamom
gongura leaves	ambadi, pundipallya, sorrel leaves
haldi	turmeric
hing	asafoetida
jaiphal	nutmeg
jaiphal patri or jaypatri	mace
jeera	cumin
karale	niger seeds
khada hing	whole asafoetida
khus khus	poppy seeds
lavang	clove
maratha moggu	dried capers
methi	fenugreek
nagkeshar	cobra saffron
phutanay or pandharpuri dal	roasted channa
rai	mustard seeds
saunf	fennel
shahajeera	black cumin
tadka	tempering with oil and other ingredients, also called phodni
tamalpatra	bay leaf
til	sesame
urad dal	black gram

Acknowledgements

This book has been a labour of love, learning and patience. We started on the book thinking that we can just get hold of an SLR camera, make a few chutneys, click some photographs, write up the story and the recipes and hand them over to a publisher! As we went and bought ten different types of chillies from the Pune market, took a few photographs and started on the recipes, we quickly realised that we needed a professional photographer to help us if we wanted to produce a professional effort. Vikas Shinde, our photographer guided us through what is required for a pictorial book and that it needs to be designed! Thank you Vikas for the wonderful photographs and the time we all spent together at your lovely studio.

Jaidev & Rashmi Ranade of designatwork, who designed the book and guided us all through the process of publishing it. Thank you for putting together the wonderful design of this book and for helping us show our well-wishers while the work was in progress, that we were serious about the book!

Gouri Dange, who was kind enough to edit our manuscript. Thanks Gouri for your focused effort that kept our enthusiasm on the book going, made the book much better, readable and consistent. Your insights kept us going.

Dr Gaddagimath of Sarpan Hybrid Seeds, Dharwad, thank you for guiding us through the science of the chilli and its wonderful facets. Without your Sudhindra Mokhasi, who helped us through the labyrinth of the publishing world and introduced us to several publishers including Rupa Publications. Thanks Sudhindra, without your help we would probably have only posted the contents of the book on an Internet BLOG!

To Shyamala and Meera Agarkhed, Lata Kulkarni, Kittu and Madhu Mokhasi and our moushis and mamas in Hubli who enthusiastically helped us with many of the traditional recipes and put us in touch with the chilli trade in North Karnataka. Arti Patil for her help with the Kolhapuri Masala recipe.

To several people who helped us in trying to find a sponsor for the book. Thank your Amar Krishnamurthy for your untiring efforts. To all our relatives, friends and well-wishers who kept asking and reminding us about the book and ensured that the book was completed and published!

To our spouses Shrikant and Padmaja and our children Pranav & Mihika and Smriti & Kriti for their patience and forbearance on our additional weekend activity that they had to bear with. Padmaja for her help with many of the recipes and locating information on traditions in North Karnataka.

Hope all of you enjoy reading this book and whip up a few chutneys for your next party!

Sunita & Sunil

References

The Conquering Chilli
Chilli, Tabasco - *Wikipedia*
A Historical Dictionary of Indian Food - *K.T. Achaya*
Mexico's long chilli love affair - *BBC Report*
Chillies Down Under - *Nigel Laubsch*
The Great Chile Book - *Mark Miller*

Facets of the Chilli
Chilli Articles of D Balasubramanian - *The Hindu*
Saga Jolokia: Indian chilli acquires cult following in US - *Chidanand Rajghatta, Times News Network*
MCX India; Commodities Exchange - *www.mcxindia.com*
Indian Spice Board - *www.indianspices.com*

Special Effects
www.chilly.in   website

Chillies of the World
Spice Board of India - *www.indianspices.com*
Work of Dr Gaddagimath, PhD, Horticultural Sciences & Chillies
Application specific chillies developed by Sarpan Hybrids
Chilli, Naga Chilli - *Wikipedia*

Chilling Cuisines of the World
Chinese Cuisine - *Wikipedia*
Thai Cuisine - *Wikipedia*
Chilli Peppers in Mexican Cuisine - *by Heleigh Bostwick*
Chiles a World Tour

About the Authors

Sunita Gogate Sunita is a veteran of the Indian and International School systems, having worked with the SSC and IB systems for many years. She is now a stay-at-home mom and loves experimenting with food from all over the world. She is interested in travelling and trying global cuisines, hosting parties and cooking exotic food.

She lives in Raleigh, North Carolina, USA with her husband Shrikant and children Pranav and Mihika.

Sunil Jalihal An IT professional who worked for Wipro, Siemens and Hewlett-Packard before becoming a technology entrepreneur, Sunil has keen interests in organic food, green technologies, heritage and history. His work and vacations have taken him to various parts of the world, where his foodie instincts have taken him on culinary adventures with local foods of many regions. He is currently working on a new venture in the mobile technology space while putting this book together and supporting various green initiatives.

He lives in Pune, India with his wife Padmaja and daughters Smriti and Kriti.